Fantastic Quilts

Bed Quilt directions on p.2

Bed Quilt p.1

Materials: Assorted cotton print scraps (1056 pieces of triangle patch). 80cm by 146cm ($31^1/2''$ × $57^1/2''$) cotton for border. 90cm by 1m ($35^3/8''$ × $39^3/8''$) cotton for binding. 76cm by 320cm ($29^7/8''$ × $126''$) backing. 76cm by 320cm ($29^7/8''$ × $126''$) batting.
Finished size: 146cm by 156cm ($57^1/2''$ × $61^3/8''$)

Directions: 1. Cut and piece 132 blocks and join pieced blocks together as shown.
2. Join border strips to pieced top lengthwise and then crosswise.
3. Place batting between pieced top and backing. Baste in place, starting at center and working outward. Quilt pieced blocks as shown.

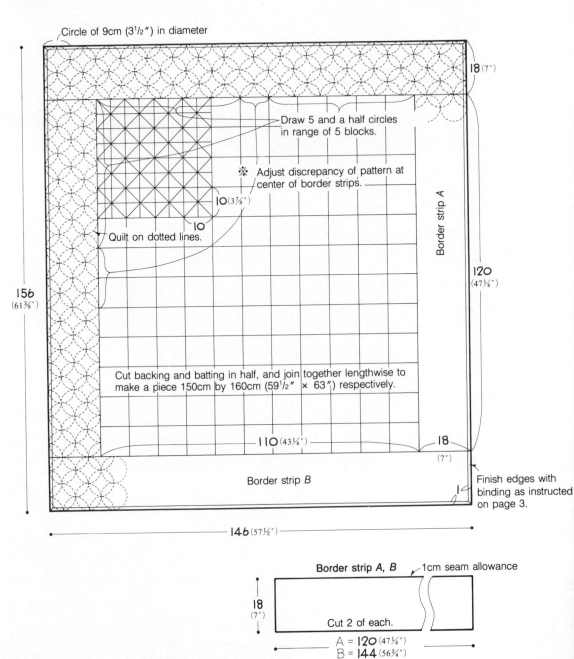

Circle of 9cm ($3^1/2''$) in diameter

18 (7")

Draw 5 and a half circles in range of 5 blocks.

※ Adjust discrepancy of pattern at center of border strips.

Border strip A

10 ($3^7/8''$)

10

Quilt on dotted lines.

120 ($47^1/4''$)

156 ($61^3/8''$)

Cut backing and batting in half, and join together lengthwise to make a piece 150cm by 160cm ($59^1/2''$ × 63") respectively.

110 ($43^1/4''$)

18 (7")

Border strip B

Finish edges with binding as instructed on page 3.

146 ($57^1/2''$)

Border strip A, B — 1cm seam allowance

18 (7")

Cut 2 of each.

A = 120 ($47^1/4''$)
B = 144 ($56^3/4''$)

Binding — '0.7cm ($1/4''$) seam allowance

2 ($3/4''$).

604 (19' $9^3/4''$)

2

4. Cut a circle template of 9cm (3¹/₂″) in diameter and match-mark as shown. Draw quilting lines, matching the marks. (Adjust discrepancy of pattern at center of border strips.)

5. Quilt border strips and finish edges with binding.

Quilting pattern for border

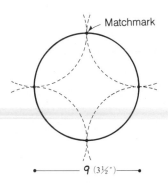

Matchmark

9 (3½″)

Piecing diagram of block

Cut 1056 triangle patch pieces for 132 blocks.

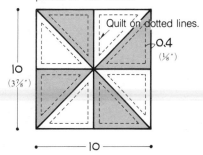

Quilt on dotted lines.

0.4 (⅛″)

10 (3⅞″)

10

0.5cm (¹/₄″) seam allowance for each

Directions for finishing

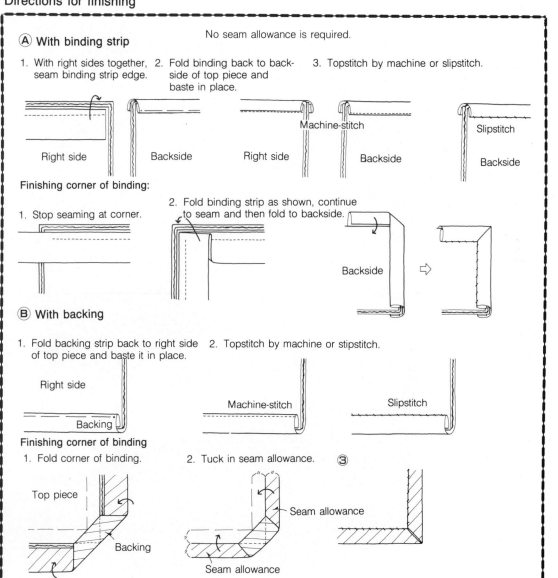

No seam allowance is required.

Ⓐ **With binding strip**

1. With right sides together, seam binding strip edge.
2. Fold binding back to backside of top piece and baste in place.
3. Topstitch by machine or slipstitch.

Right side   Backside   Right side   Machine-stitch   Backside   Slipstitch   Backside

Finishing corner of binding:

1. Stop seaming at corner.
2. Fold binding strip as shown, continue to seam and then fold to backside.

Backside

Ⓑ **With backing**

1. Fold backing strip back to right side of top piece and baste it in place.
2. Topstitch by machine or stipstitch.

Right side

Backing

Machine-stitch   Slipstitch

Finishing corner of binding

1. Fold corner of binding.
2. Tuck in seam allowance.   ③

Top piece

Backing

Seam allowance

Seam allowance

Fantastic Quilts

Bed Quilt and Pillowcase directions on p.6

Bed Quilt and Pillowcase pp.4,5

Bed Quilt

Materials: Assorted cotton print scraps (780 pieces of 8.4cm (3¹/₄″) square patch). 93cm by 424cm (36⁵/₈″ × 166⁷/₈″) backing. 92cm by 40cm (36¹/₄″ × 15³/₄″) binding. 120cm by 424cm (47¹/₄″ × 166⁷/₈″) batting.

Finished size: 184cm by 212cm (72³/₈″ × 83¹/₂″)
Directions: Cut and join patch pieces together. Place batting between pieced top and backing, and quilt. Finish edges with binding strips *a* and *b*.

Seam allowance for patch piece is 0.7cm (¹/₄″).
Seam allowance for binding strip is 1cm (³/₈″).

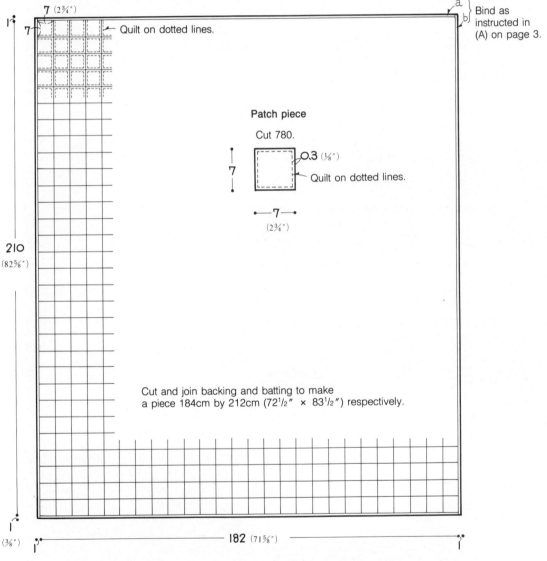

7 (2¾″)

Quilt on dotted lines.

a
b } Bind as instructed in (A) on page 3.

Patch piece

Cut 780.

0.3 (⅛″)

Quilt on dotted lines.

7

—7—
(2¾″)

210
(82⅝″)

Cut and join backing and batting to make a piece 184cm by 212cm (72¹/₂″ × 83¹/₂″) respectively.

(³/₈″)

182 (71⅝″)

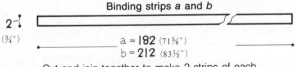

Binding strips *a* and *b*

2
(¾″)

a = 182 (71⅝″)
b = 212 (83½″)

Cut and join together to make 2 strips of each.

Pillowcase

Materials: Assorted cotton print scraps (34 pieces of 8.4cm (3¹/₄″) square patch). 90cm by 153cm (35³/₈″ × 60¹/₄″) light orange cotton.
Finished size: 84cm by 49cm (33¹/₁₆″ × 19¹/₄″)
Directions: 1. Cut and join patch pieces as shown.
2. Lay pieced top on right side of front piece, and top-stitch or quilt on dotted lines.

3. Hem one edge of back piece and flap piece respectively. With wrong side of back piece and right side of flap piece together, overlapping 20cm (7⁷/₈″) as shown, and baste.
4. With right sides of top and back pieces together, seam and turn right sides out.

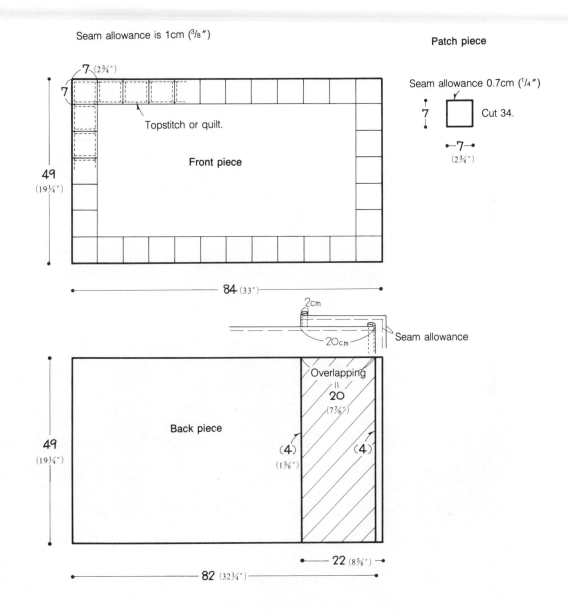

Seam allowance is 1cm (³/₈″)

Patch piece

7 (2¾″)

7

Topstitch or quilt.

Front piece

49
(19¼″)

84 (33″)

Seam allowance 0.7cm (¹/₄″)

7

Cut 34.

7
(2¾″)

2cm

20cm

Seam allowance

Overlapping
||
20
(7⅞″)

Back piece

49
(19¼″)

(4)
(1⅝″)

(4)

22 (8⅝″)

82 (32¼″)

Mat directions on p.10   **Basket Cover** directions on p.66

Fantastic Quilts

Mat pp.8,9

Materials: 18cm by 212cm ($7^1/_{16}$″ × $83^1/_2$″) dark cotton print. 18cm by 212cm ($7^1/_{16}$″ × $83^1/_2$″) light cotton print. 4 strips of 15cm by 212cm ($5^7/_8$″ × $83^1/_2$″) dark cotton print. 15cm by 212cm ($5^7/_8$″ × $83^1/_2$″) light cotton print. 60 pieces of dark large triangle patch. 54 pieces of light large triangle patch. 12 pieces of light small triangle patch. 90cm by 130cm ($35^3/_8$″ × $51^1/_8$″) dark cotton print for binding.

90cm by 440cm ($35^3/_8$″ × $173^1/_4$″) backing.
Finished size: 212cm by 162cm ($83^1/_2$″ × $63^3/_4$″)
Directions: Join triangle patch pieces to make strips, and then join strips as shown. Place batting between top piece and backing, quilt as shown and trim batting and backing to size of top piece. Finish edges with binding.

1cm ($^3/_8$″) seam allowance

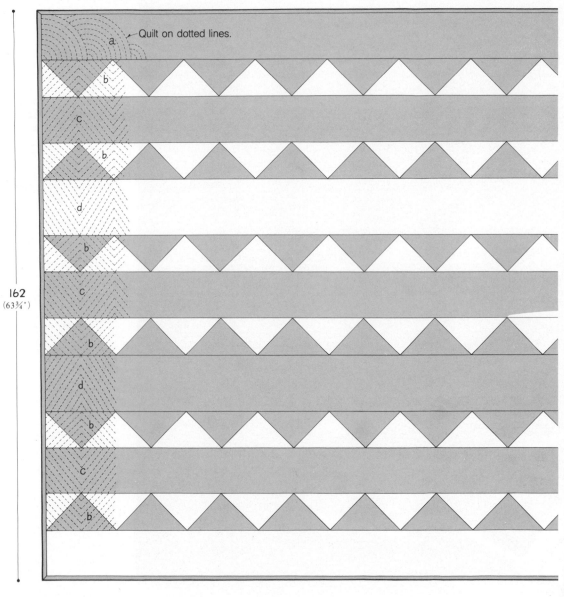

162 ($63^3/_4$″)

212$^{(83^1/_2″)}$

Triangle patch piece

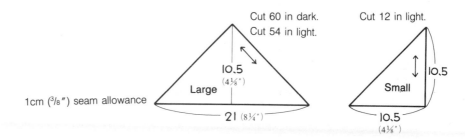

Cut 60 in dark.
Cut 54 in light.

Cut 12 in light.

Large 10.5 (4⅛")
21 (8¼")
1cm (³/₈") seam allowance

Small 10.5
10.5 (4⅛")

Quilting pattern

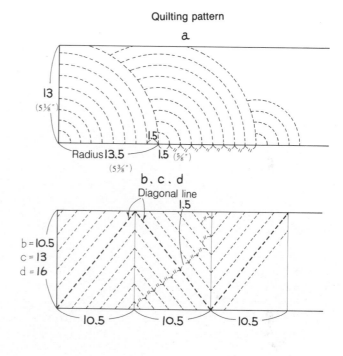

a

13 (5⅛")
1.5
Radius 13.5 (5⅜")
1.5 (⅝")

b、c、d

Diagonal line
1.5
b = 10.5
c = 13
d = 16
10.5   10.5   10.5

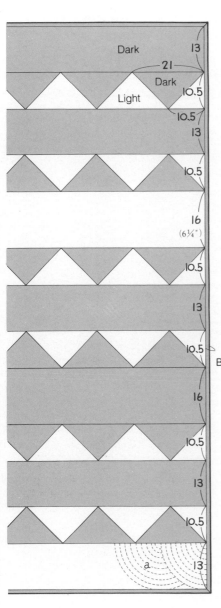

Dark   13
21
Dark   10.5
Light
10.5
13
10.5
16 (6¼")
10.5
13
10.5
16
10.5
13
10.5
a   13

Bind as instructed in (A) on page 3.

* Make bias strip of 4cm by 750cm (1⅝" × 295¼") for binding.

Cut and join batting and backing to make a piece
220cm by 170cm (86⅝" × 66⅞") respectively.

Joining

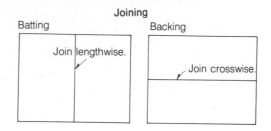

Batting
Join lengthwise.

Backing
Join crosswise.

Living Room Wonders

A

B

Coverlet Quilt directions on p.14   **Cushions A and B** directions on p.69

13

Coverlet Quilt pp.12,13

Materials: 140cm by 160cm ($55^1/8'' \times 63''$) solid charcoal gray woolen. 140cm by 1m ($55^1/8'' \times 39^3/8''$) red checkered woolen. 140cm by 50cm ($55^1/8'' \times 19^5/8''$) light brown checkered woolen. 140cm by 50cm ($55^1/8'' \times 19^5/8''$) white checkered woolen. 92cm by 370cm ($36^1/4'' \times 145^5/8''$) black velour. 180cm ($70^7/8''$) long zipper. 9 skeins of off-white embroidery floss.

Finished size: 180cm ($70^7/8''$) square

Directions: Cut 18 pieces of charcoal gray woolen and embroider each piece as shown. Cut and join patch pieces (*a*, *b*, *c* and *d*) as shown. Sew on zipper. With right sides together, seam pieced top and back piece and turn right sides out.

In joining embroidered pieces, note the direction of their upper and lower sides (as indicated by the direction of a in piecing diagram).

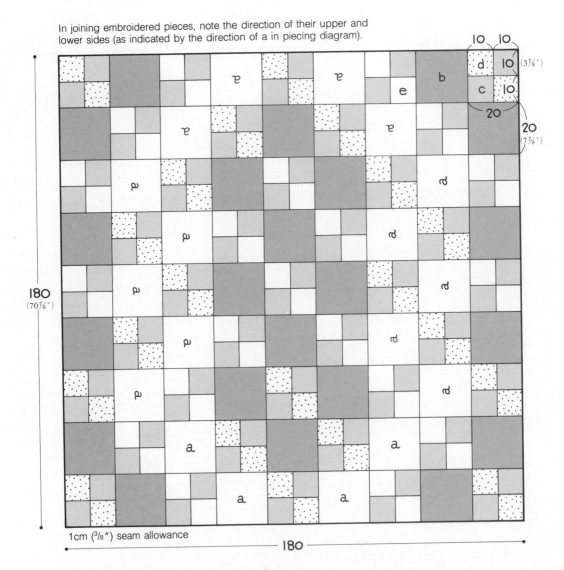

1cm ($^3/8''$) seam allowance

Cut and join backing to make a 182cm ($71^5/8''$) square piece.

Cutting
a (embroidered): Cut 18 in solid charcoal gray.
b: Cut 22 in solid charcoal gray.
c: Cut 82 in red checkered.
d: Cut 42 in light brown checkered.
e: Cut 40 in white checkered.

Embroidery pattern (actual size)

Use 6 strands of embroidery floss, and embroider
with outline stitch unless otherwise specified.

French knot

Satin stitch

Straight stitch

Fly stitch

Straight stitch

Living Room Wonders

Cushions A, B, C, D and E directions on pp.18,19

Patchwork Picture directions on p.67

Cushions A, B and C pp. 16, 17

Materials: *A*: 90cm by 180cm (35³/₈″ × 70⁷/₈″) unbleached muslin; 40cm by 10cm (15³/₄″ × 3⁷/₈″) print cotton *#1*; 80cm by 40cm (31¹/₂″ × 15³/₄″) print cotton *#2*. *B*: 48cm (18⁷/₈″) square unbleached muslin; 80cm by 40cm (31¹/₂″ × 15³/₄″) print cotton *#1*; 75cm by 60cm (29¹/₂″ × 23⁵/₈″) print cotton *#3*; 90cm (35³/₈″) square print cotton *#4*. *C*: 90cm by 180cm (35³/₈″ × 70⁷/₈″) striped cotton; 80cm by 50cm (31¹/₂″ × 19⁵/₈″) checkered cotton. For each: Ready-made round inner cushion; 30cm (11³/₄″) long zipper.

Finished size: 30cm (11³/₄″) in diameter (not including binding)

Directions: 1. Cut decorative print square (a, b, c and d) and fold them as shown. Lay 4 folded pieces for each print square in indicated sequence on foundation fabric, basting each piece in place.

2. Stich by machine on octasector dotted lines as shown. Trim edges of foundation to circle of 31.4cm (12³/₈″) in diameter.

3. Sew on zipper to back piece.

4. With wrong sides of top and back pieces together, finish edge with binding.

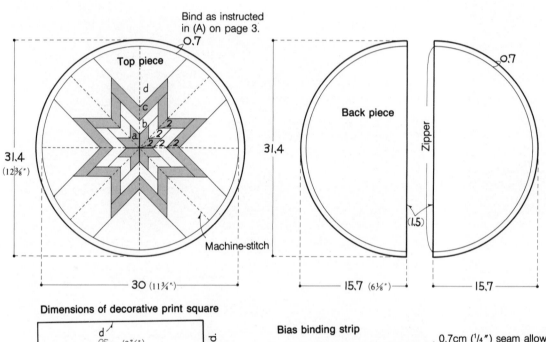

Bind as instructed in (A) on page 3.

Top piece

Machine-stitch

Back piece

Zipper

31.4 (12³/₈″)

30 (11³/₄″)

15.7 (6¹/₈″) 15.7

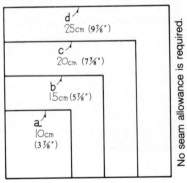

Dimensions of decorative print square

d 25cm (9⁷/₈″)
c 20cm (7⁷/₈″)
b 15cm (5⁷/₈″)
a 10cm (3⁷/₈″)

No seam allowance is required.

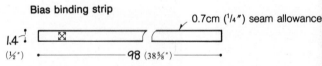

Bias binding strip

0.7cm (¹/₄″) seam allowance

1.4 (½″)   98 (38⁵/₈″)

Cut foundation fabric to make a piece 48cm (18⁷/₈″) square, lay decorative pieces on it, machine-stitch in place and then trim edges to circle of 31.4cm (12³/₈″) in diameter.

Cutting and color scheme

		A:	B:	C:
Foundation:	1	unbleached,	unbleached,	striped
Dec. print a:	4	print #1,	print #3,	checkered
Dec. print b:	8	unbleached,	print #4,	striped
Dec. print c:	8	print #2,	print #1,	checkered
Dec. print d:	8	unbleached,	each 4 of print #3 and #4	striped
Back piece:	2	unbleached,	print #3,	striped
Binding strip:	1	unbleached,	print #4,	striped

18

Laying decorative prints

1. Fold square print piece as shown.

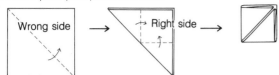

4. Lay remaining 4 pieces of print *b* between the laid pieces of print *b* respectively in 2cm ($^3/_4$″) from center, and baste them in place. Lay print *c* and *d* pieces in the same way on octasector lines every 2cm from center.

2. Draw octasector line on foundation piece, lay 4 pieces of print *a* in center, and baste them in place.

3. Lay 4 pieces of print *b* in 2cm ($^3/_4$″) from center, and baste.

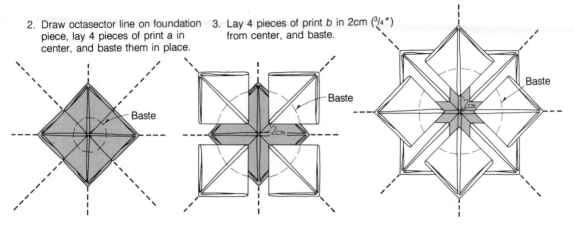

Cushions D and E   p.16

Materials: *D*: 90cm by 45cm ($35^3/_8$″ × $17^3/_4$″) blue-gray denim; 85cm ($33^1/_2$″) of 4.5cm ($1^3/_4$″) wide white gathered lace. *E*: 90cm by 32cm ($35^3/_8$″ × $12^5/_8$″) brown hemp; 26cm by 7cm ($10^1/_4$″ × $2^3/_4$″) olive-green print cotton; 72cm by 13cm ($28^2/_3$″ × $5^1/_8$″) light brown cotton.
For *D* and *E*: One 30cm ($11^3/_4$″) square inner cushion each; 30cm long zipper; Synthetic filler. **Finished size:** 30cm ($11^3/_4$″) square

Seam allowance is 1cm ($^3/_8$″) except for patch pieces and given in parentheses.

Continued on page 78.

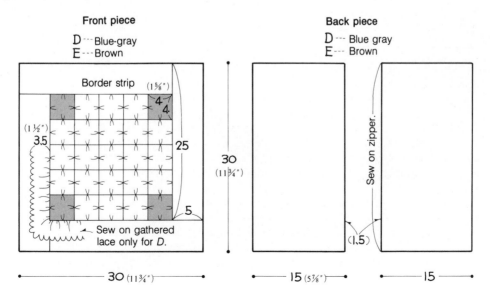

Lap Quilt directions on p.22 **Cushions** directions on p.23

Living Room Wonders

Runner directions on p.22

Lap Quilt p.20

Materials: 90cm by 60cm (35³/₈″ × 32⁵/₈″) dark gray cotton, 90cm by 60cm medium gray cotton, 90cm by 60cm light gray cotton, 90cm by 230cm (35³/₈″ × 90¹/₂″) off-white cotton (includes backing and binding).

Finished size: 162cm by 82cm (63³/₄″ × 32¹/₄″)
Directions: Cut and join patch pieces (a, b, c and d) as shown on piecing diagram. With wrong sides of pieced top and backing together, finish edges with binding.

1cm (³/₈″) seam allowance

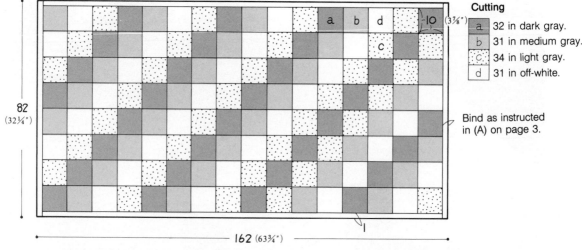

82
(32¼″)

162 (63¾″)

Cutting

a	32 in dark gray.
b	31 in medium gray.
c	34 in light gray.
d	31 in off-white.

Bind as instructed in (A) on page 3.

Cut backing to make a piece 86cm by 166cm (33⁷/₈″ × 65³/₈″).

Runner p.21

Materials: 45cm by 128cm (17³/₄″ × 50³/₈″) solid gray cotton (includes patch pieces). Assorted gray striped and checkered cotton scraps (64 patch pieces).
Finished size: 123cm by 33cm (48³/₈″ × 13″)

Directions: Cut and join 12cm by 7cm (4³/₄″ × 2³/₄″) patch pieces as shown, and quilt. With wrong sides of pieced top and backing together, finish edges with binding.

1cm (³/₈″) seam allowance

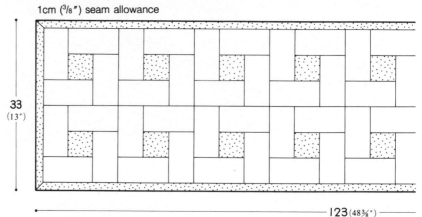

33
(13″)

123 (48³/₈″)

※ ▦ Cut 16 in solid gray.

b, c, d and e: Cut 64 in total in gray-striped and -checkered.
Cut backing to make a piece 38cm by 128cm (15″ × 50³/₈″).

Cushions p.20

Materials for 1 cushion: 36cm by 12cm ($14^1/8'' \times 4^3/4''$) of 3 assorted gray checkered cotton, 48cm by 12cm ($18^7/8'' \times 4^3/4''$) gray wide-striped cotton, 60cm by 12cm ($23^5/8'' \times 4^3/4''$) gray pin-striped cotton. 90cm by 50cm ($35^3/8'' \times 19^5/8''$) cotton (Left: light gray, Right: off-white). 40cm ($15^3/4''$) square inner cushion.

Finished size: 40cm ($15^3/4''$) square

Directions: Cut and join patch pieces (*a*, *b* and *c*). With right side together, matching marks, sew along raw edges, leaving opening for stuffing. Turn right side out, stuff with inner cushion and seam opening with blindstitch.

Cutting

Left and Right:
   a: Cut 3 in large-checkered.
       Cut 3 in medium-checkered.
       Cut 3 in small-checkered.
       Cut 4 in wide-striped.
       Cut 5 in pin-striped.
Left:
   b: Cut 36 in light gray.
   c: Cut 16 in light gray.
Right:
   b: Cut 36 in off-white.
   c: Cut 16 in off-white.

1cm ($^3/8''$) seam allowance

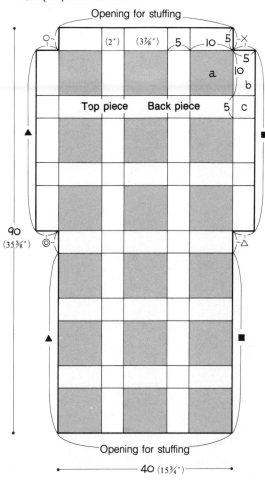

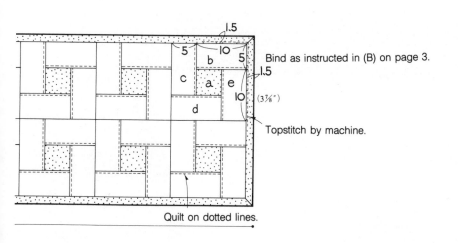

Bind as instructed in (B) on page 3.

Topstitch by machine.

Quilt on dotted lines.

My Favorite Things

Lap Quilt directions on p.26

Lap Quilt p.24

Materials: 90cm by 80cm (35³/₈″ × 31¹/₂″) dark brown cotton. 90cm by 151cm (35³/₈″ × 59¹/₂″) white cotton. 62cm by 34cm (24³/₈″ × 13³/₈″) blue-gray cotton. Assorted cotton scraps for applique and patch pieces. 90cm by 162cm (35³/₈″ × 63³/₄″) batting. Embroidery floss: small amount each of brown, dark pink, light blue, dark brown, green, dark gray, beige, blue, white, dark blue and olive-green. White and dark brown quilting thread.

Finished size: 90cm by 81cm (35³/₈″ × 31⁷/₈″)

Directions: 1. Applique wall, chimney and roof to foundation, and quilt as shown.

2. Applique window frame and door to foundation. Applique and embroider to door piece as shown on page 27.

3. Make up shopwindow pieces and signboard piece as instructed on pages 74 - 77, and applique them to foundation. Embroider chimney piece.
4. Cut and join patch pieces to make 4 blocks.
5. Join dark brown border strips and blocks to foundation piece.
6. Place 2 pieces of batting between top piece and backing, baste it and quilt around window frame, signboard, wall and foundation pieces respectively.
7. Quilt dark brown border and corner blocks as shown.
8. Bind edges of top piece with backing.

Cut white backing to make a piece 94cm by 85cm (37″ × 33¹/₂″).
Cut batting to make 2 pieces 90cm by 81cm (35³/₈″ × 31⁷/₈″).

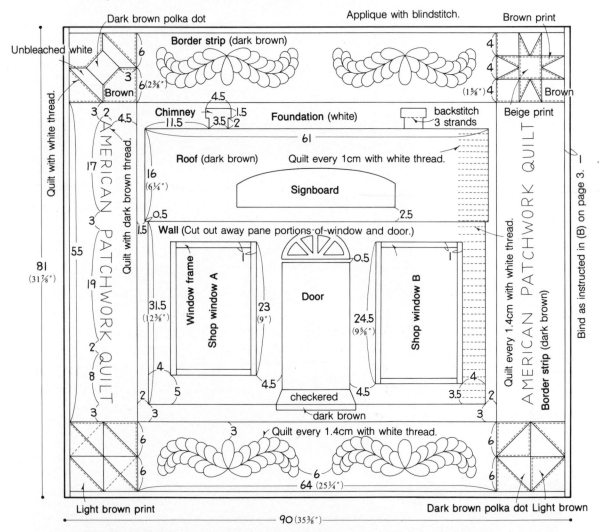

Border: 66cm by 14cm (26″ × 5¹/₂″) Cut 2 in dark brown.
57cm by 14cm (22¹/₂″ × 5¹/₂″) Cut 2 in dark brown.
Foundation: 66cm by 57cm (26″ × 22¹/₂″) Cut 1 in white.

Door piece (actual size)

Cut applique pieces, adding 0.5cm (¹/₄″) seam allowance   Applique with blindstitch.

Dark brown

Backstitch 3 strands brown

Backstitch 3 strands light blue

Satin stitch 2 strands white

Dark brown

White

Outline stitch 3 strands light blue

Light blue

OPEN

A.M.   P.M.
10:00 ～ 6:00

Back stitch 2 strands blue
French knot 2 strands blue

Checkered

Dark brown

Continued on page 74.

Eyeglass Case directions on p.30   **Book Cover** directions on p.31

Lampshade directions on p.79

My Favorite Things

Eyeglass Case p.28

Materials: 19cm by 15cm ($7^1/_2$″ × $5^7/_8$″) beige print cotton, 19cm by 15cm pink striped cotton, 19cm by 15cm white print cotton. 38cm by 17cm (15″ × $6^3/_4$″) batting. 17cm ($6^3/_4$″) long zipper.

Directions: 1. Cut and seam 26 patch strips (*a, b* and *c*) to foundation batting in sequence as shown on piecing diagram.
2. Lay pieced top on batting and quilt as shown.
3. With right side together, fold fabric for inner liner in half, seam sides and lower corners to provide with gore as shown.
4. Finish upper edge of top piece with binding (*A*), seaming zipper together.
5. Fold top piece in half and finish sides with binding (*B*), and seam lower corners to provide with gore as shown.
6. Put inner liner into top piece, and finish upper edge with blindstitch.

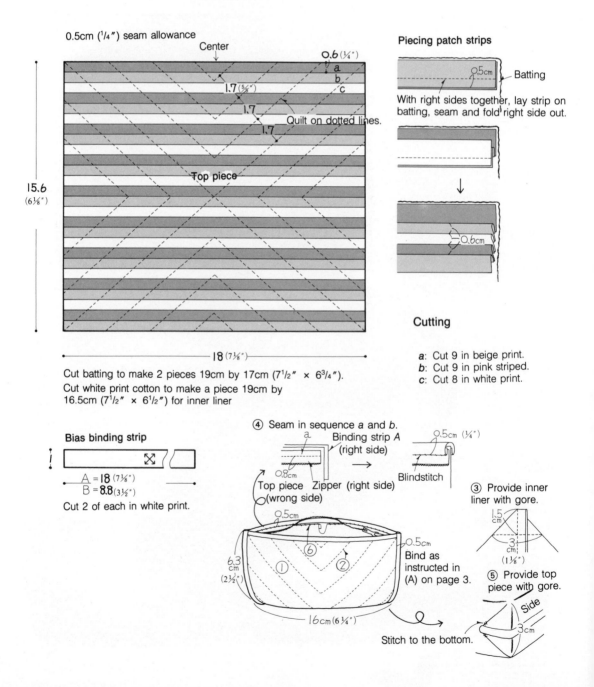

0.5cm (¼″) seam allowance

Center

0.6 (¼″)
a
b
c

1.7 (⅝″)

1.7

1.7

Quilt on dotted lines.

Top piece

15.6 (6⅛″)

18 (7⅛″)

Cut batting to make 2 pieces 19cm by 17cm ($7^1/_2$″ × $6^3/_4$″).
Cut white print cotton to make a piece 19cm by 16.5cm ($7^1/_2$″ × $6^1/_2$″) for inner liner

Piecing patch strips

0.5cm — Batting

With right sides together, lay strip on batting, seam and fold right side out.

0.6cm

Cutting

a: Cut 9 in beige print.
b: Cut 9 in pink striped.
c: Cut 8 in white print.

Bias binding strip

A = 18 (7⅛″)
B = 8.8 (3½″)

Cut 2 of each in white print.

④ Seam in sequence *a* and *b*.

a   Binding strip A (right side)

0.5cm (¼″)

0.8cm

Top piece   Zipper (right side) (wrong side)

Blindstitch

③ Provide inner liner with gore.

1.5 cm
3 cm (1⅛″)

0.5cm

6.3 cm (2½″)

① ⑥ ②

0.5cm

Bind as instructed in (A) on page 3.

⑤ Provide top piece with gore.

Side

3cm

16cm (6¼″)

Stitch to the bottom.

Book Cover p.28

Materials: *Left*: 90cm by 42cm (35³/₈″ × 16¹/₂″) striped print cotton; 24cm by 4cm (9¹/₂″ × 1⁵/₈″) moss-green print cotton; 24cm by 4cm unbleached print cotton; 15cm by 21cm (5⁷/₈″ × 8¹/₄″) batting; 15cm by 4cm backing; 45cm by 21cm (17³/₄″ × 8¹/₄″) adhesive padding. *Right*: 90cm by 26cm (35³/₈″ × 10¹/₄″) beige print cotton; 31cm (12¹/₄″) square black print cotton; 24cm by 4cm unbleached print cotton; 15cm by 21cm batting; 15cm by 21cm backing; 45cm by 21cm adhesive padding.

Directions: 1. Cut and join patch pieces to make front piece A.

2. Place batting between front piece *A* and backing, quilt and join it to front piece *B*.

3. Put adhesive padding on one piece of lapel. With right sides together, seam long end of lapel pieces, turn right sides out and topstitch along seamed edge by machine.

4. Put adhesive padding on back piece. With right sides of front and back pieces together, seam end of portion for folding back, turn right sides out and topstitch along seamed edge by machine. Topstitch on seamline of front pieces *A* and *B* by machine.

5. Lay lapel on back piece and finish raw edge with binding strip *A* as shown.

6. Lay strap on back piece and finish upper and lower edges with binding strip *B*.

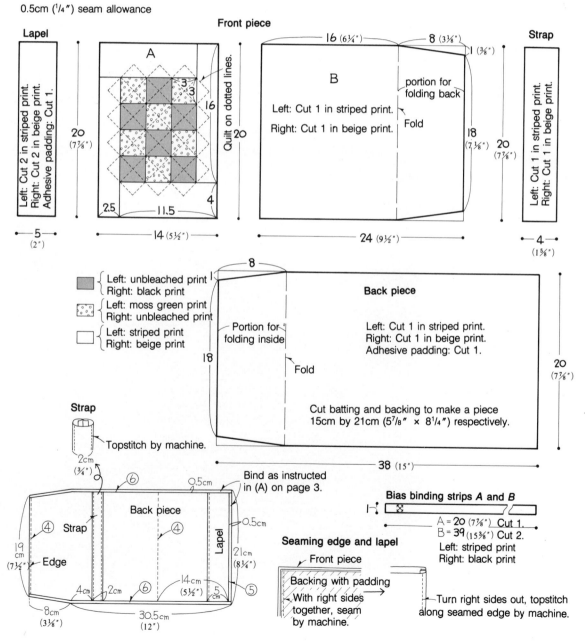

0.5cm (¹/₄″) seam allowance

My Favorite Things

A (Basket Cover) directions on p.34

(Basket) directions on p.35   **Pincushions** directions on p.80

33

Basket Cover p.32

Materials: 13.5cm by 18cm ($5^{1}/_{4}$" × $7^{1}/_{16}$") white cotton, 30cm ($11^{3}/_{4}$") square dark brown print, 11cm by 7cm ($4^{3}/_{8}$" × $2^{3}/_{4}$") off-white cotton, 7cm by 4cm ($2^{3}/_{4}$" × $1^{5}/_{8}$") light brown print, 7cm by 4cm beige print. Embroidery floss: Small amount each of black, red and wine-red. Black cotton thread. 8cm ($3^{1}/_{8}$") of 2cm ($3^{/}_{4}$") wide white cotton lace. 8cm of 2cm wide cream-colored tulle lace. 6cm ($2^{3}/_{8}$") of 0.3cm ($1^{/}_{8}$") wide green satin ribbon, 6cm of 0.3cm wide gray satin ribbon. 2 pearl-beads of 0.3cm in diameter. 13.5cm by 9cm ($5^{3}/_{8}$" × $3^{1}/_{2}$") batting. Synthetic filler.

Directions: Applique to top piece. Place batting between top piece and backing, and finish edges with binding. Sew on a loop to handle of basket as shown.

4
2
4 ($1^{5}/_{8}$")
0.8

9
($3^{1}/_{2}$")

Top piece: Cut 1 in white.
Back piece: Cut 1 in white.
Batting: Cut 1.

No seam allowance is required.

Bind as instructed in (A) on page 3.

13.5 ($5^{3}/_{8}$")

Make 3.2cm by 39cm ($1^{1}/_{4}$" × $15^{3}/_{8}$") bias strip for binding in dark brown print.
Make 2.5cm by 6cm (1" × $2^{3}/_{8}$") bias strip for loop in dark brown print.

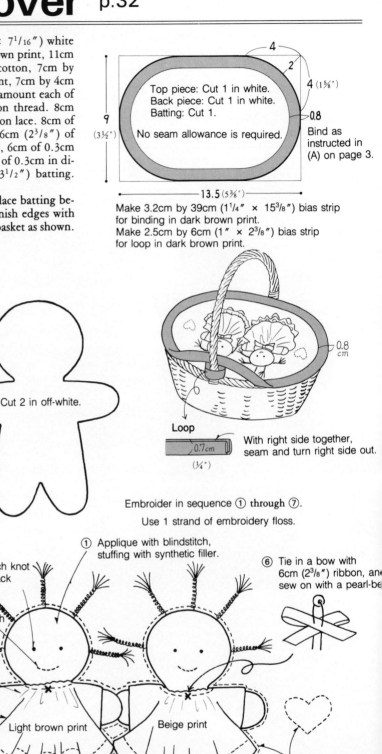

Applique pattern (actual size)

0.5cm ($1^{/}_{4}$") seam allowance

⑤ Embroider face and feet, and set hairs.

Cut 2 in off-white.

Braiding hair

4 strands of black cotton thread

Braid and tie.

1.5cm ($5^{/}_{8}$")

Loop

0.7cm
($1^{/}_{4}$")

With right side together, seam and turn right side out.

Embroider in sequence ① through ⑦.
Use 1 strand of embroidery floss.

① Applique with blindstitch, stuffing with synthetic filler.

⑥ Tie in a bow with 6cm ($2^{3}/_{8}$") ribbon, and sew on with a pearl-be

French knot in black

Backstitch in red

③ Hem lower edge of 7cm by 4cm ($2^{3}/_{4}$" × $1^{5}/_{8}$") print. Fold other edges 0.5cm ($1^{/}_{4}$") back, and gather upper edge with running stitch.

Light brown print

Beige print

④ Tuck to shape of one-piece dress, applique it with blindstitch and stitch to lace in a few points.

Cotton lace

Tulle lace

⑦ Place batting betwe top piece and back and quilt on dotted

② Sew on 8cm ($3^{1}/_{8}$") gathered lace.

Satin stitch in wine-red
Backstitch in wine-red

Basket p.33

Materials: 18cm by 40cm (7⅞" × 15¾") striped print cotton. 90cm by 10cm (35⅜" × 3⅞") dark red cotton. 40cm by 5cm (15¾" × 2") red checkered cotton. 27cm (10⅝") square off-white print. 34cm by 12cm (13⅜" × 4¾") batting. Synthetic filler. 8 small bells.

Directions: 1. Cut and join 2 patch pieces in striped print and 1 patch piece in checkered to make 4 blocks.

2. Join blocks and bottom piece to make outer piece.

3. With right sides together, seam outer and inner pieces, leaving an opening for stuffing, and turn right sides out.

4. Topstitch on seamline of bottom and 3 side pieces by machine, leaving one side open. Stuff with synthetic filler and topstitch on remaining seamline.

5. Topstitch on seamline of outer piece, and stuff with synthetic filler.

6. Finish raw edges of side pieces with binding, laying batting between as shown.

7. Tuck in raw edges of binding strips, seam edges with blindstitch, and put a bell to each ends of binding strips. Tie strips in a bow.

8. Make up a handle strap and sew on as shown.

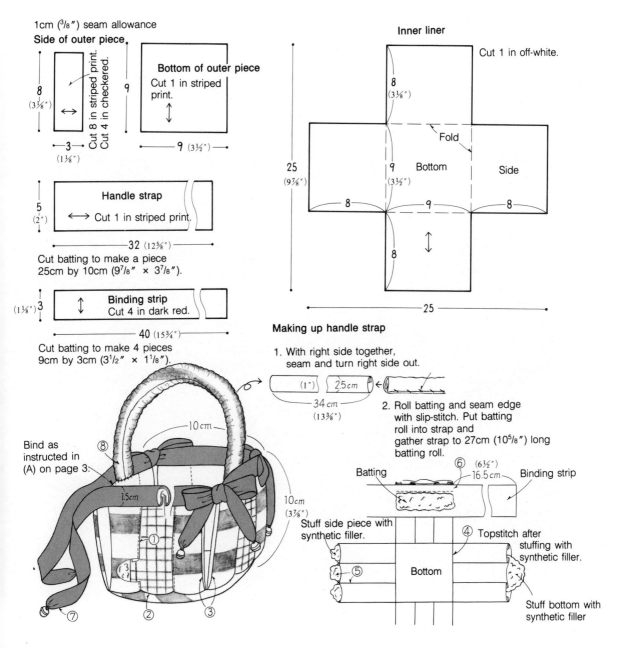

1cm (⅜") seam allowance

Side of outer piece

8 (3⅛") — 3 (1⅛")

Cut 8 in striped print. Cut 4 in checkered.

9

Bottom of outer piece
Cut 1 in striped print.

9 (3½")

Handle strap
← Cut 1 in striped print.

5 (2")

32 (12⅜")

Cut batting to make a piece 25cm by 10cm (9⅞" × 3⅞").

Binding strip
Cut 4 in dark red.

(1⅛") 3

40 (15¾")

Cut batting to make 4 pieces 9cm by 3cm (3½" × 1⅛").

Inner liner

Cut 1 in off-white.

8 (3⅛")

Fold

25 (9⅞")

9 (3½") Bottom   Side

8   9   8

8

25

Making up handle strap

1. With right side together, seam and turn right side out.

(1") — 25cm
34cm (13⅜")

2. Roll batting and seam edge with slip-stitch. Put batting roll into strap and gather strap to 27cm (10⅝") long batting roll.

Batting   ⑥ (6½")
16.5cm — Binding strip

Bind as instructed in (A) on page 33.

⑧

10cm

1.5cm

①

③

10cm (3⅞")

Stuff side piece with synthetic filler.

④ Topstitch after stuffing with synthetic filler.

⑤   Bottom

Stuff bottom with synthetic filler

⑦   ②   ③

Bags A,B,C,D and E directions on pp.81,83,84,38,39,respectively

36

B

C

My Favorite Things

Bag D p.36

Materials: 33cm by 55cm (13″ × 21⁵/₈″) black cotton. Checkered cotton scrap. 29cm by 54cm (11³/₈″ × 21¹/₄″) backing. 20cm (7⁷/₈″) zipper. 150cm of black synthetic leather rope (0.7cm in diameter). 2 sets of black rivet.

Directions: 1. Place batting between top piece and backing, and quilt as shown.
2. Finish upper and lower edges of outer piece with binding.
3. Sew on zipper close to binding.

4. Cut and join patch pieces to make top piece for round end piece.
5. Stitch along raw edges of outer piece and gather. Baste round end top piece to gathered end, tucking in edges and setting a loop made of black synthetic leather rope, and topstitch along edge by machine.
6. Baste backing for end piece to wrong side of outer piece and blindstitch.
7. Put 130cm (51¹/₈″) long rope through loops and set with rivets.

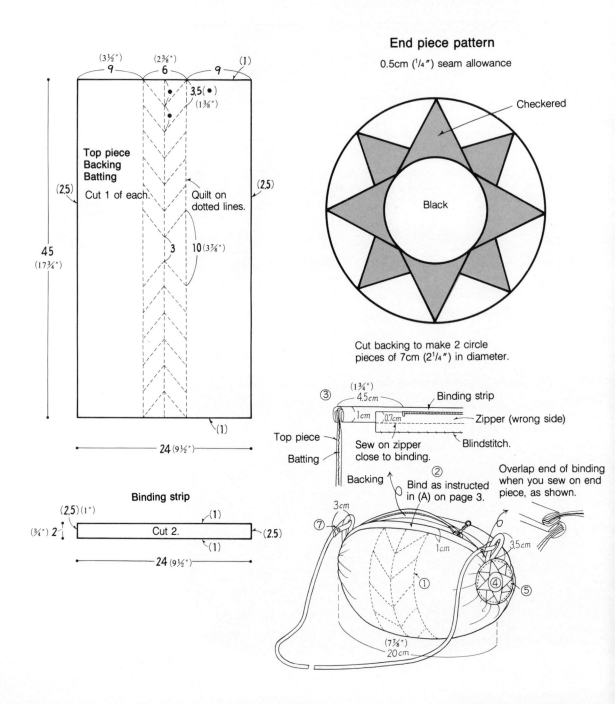

End piece pattern

0.5cm (¹/₄″) seam allowance

Checkered

Black

Cut backing to make 2 circle pieces of 7cm (2¹/₄″) in diameter.

Top piece
Backing
Batting

Cut 1 of each.

Quilt on dotted lines.

(2.5)   (2.5)

45 (17¾″)

9 (3½″)   6 (2⅜″)   9   (1)

3.5(•) (1⅜″)

3   10(3⅞″)

(1)

24 (9½″)

Binding strip

(2.5)(1″)
(¾″) 2   Cut 2.   (2.5)
(1)   (1)

24 (9½″)

③ (1¾″) 4.5cm   Binding strip
1cm   0.7cm   Zipper (wrong side)
Top piece   Sew on zipper   Blindstitch.
Batting   close to binding.
Backing   ② Bind as instructed in (A) on page 3.
Overlap end of binding when you sew on end piece, as shown.
3cm
⑦   1cm   3.5cm
①   ④   ⑤
(7⅞″) 20cm

38

Bag E p.36

Materials: 50cm by 20cm (19⁵/₈″ × 7³/₄″) black cotton. 9cm by 7cm (3¹/₂″ × 2³/₄″) checkered cotton. 9cm by 7cm striped cotton. 22cm by 7cm (8⁵/₈″ × 2³/₄″) brown checkered cotton. 27cm by 14cm (10⁵/₈″ × 5¹/₂″) backing. 24cm by 12cm (9¹/₂″ × 4³/₄″) batting. 40cm (15³/₄″) of black-and-golden lamé rope (0.3cm (¹/₈″) in diameter); 6 sets of eyelet (0.4cm in bore diameter).

Directions: 1. Cut and join patch pieces to make front and back pieces.
2. Place batting between front piece and backing, and quilt by machine. Quilt back piece in the same way, and trim side edges.
3. With right sides of front and back pieces together, seam along side and lower edges, and finish seamed edge by binding with backing of back piece.
4. Finish upper edge with binding, set on eyelets and put a rope through them.

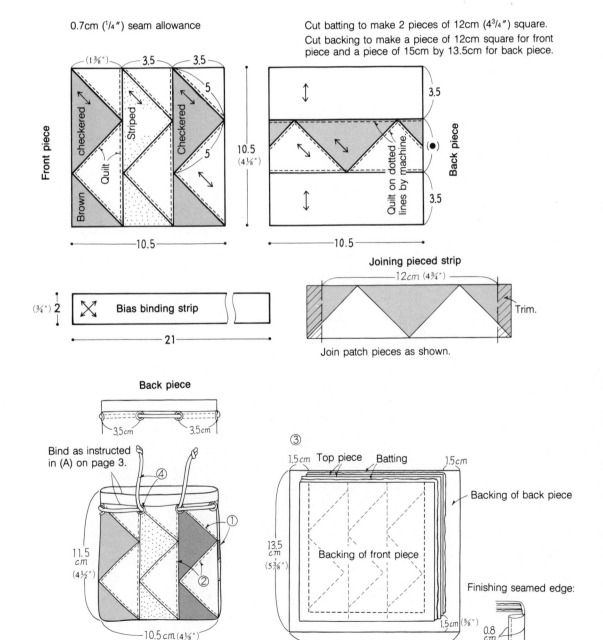

0.7cm (¹/₄″) seam allowance

Cut batting to make 2 pieces of 12cm (4³/₄″) square.
Cut backing to make a piece of 12cm square for front piece and a piece of 15cm by 13.5cm for back piece.

39

Congratulations on your baby's birth

1987

Hello, Sweet Baby

Crib Quilt directions on p.42   Photo Album Cover directions on p.85

Crib Quilt p.40

Materials: *For top piece and backing:* 75cm by 124cm (29^1/$_2$″ × 48^7/$_8$″) white-and-salmon pink print cotton; 90cm by 21cm (39^3/$_8$″ × 8^1/$_4$″) salmon pink cotton (includes binding). *For patch pieces:* 80cm by 7cm (31^1/$_2$″ × 2^3/$_4$″) white-and-salmon pink polka dot cotton; 80cm by 7cm (31^1/$_2$″ × 2^3/$_4$″) tartan cotton; 18cm by 5cm (7^1/$_8$″ × 2″) salmon pink print cotton. *For applique:* 22cm by 16cm (8^5/$_8$″ × 7^1/$_{16}$″) polka dot cotton; 16cm by 10cm (6^1/$_8$″ × 3^7/$_8$″) print cotton; 10cm (3^7/$_8$″) square of print cotton; Scrap of gingham; Scrap of skin-colored felt; 90cm by 62cm (39^3/$_8$″ × 24^3/$_8$″) batting; Synthetic filler; Red medium-fine woolen yarn; Embroidery floss:

Small amount each of salmon pink, light brown and red.

Finished size: 75cm by 62cm (29^1/$_2$″ × 24^3/$_8$″)

Directions: 1. Applique baby-in-cradle design to top piece as shown.

2. Place batting between top piece and backing, quilt along edges of applique as shown, and embroider top piece with letters.

3. Cut and join patch pieces to make 4 blocks, lay blocks on four corners of top piece, and quilt as shown.

4. Finish edges with binding.

No seam allowance is required.

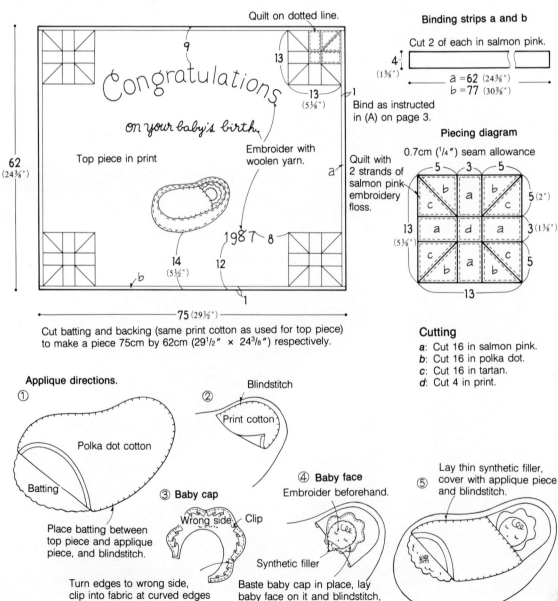

Quilt on dotted line.

Congratulations

on your baby's birth.

Top piece in print

Embroider with woolen yarn.

1987

9 13 13 1

62 (24^3/$_8$″)

14 (5^1/$_2$″) 12 8

1

75 (29^1/$_2$″)

Cut batting and backing (same print cotton as used for top piece) to make a piece 75cm by 62cm (29^1/$_2$″ × 24^3/$_8$″) respectively.

Binding strips a and b

Cut 2 of each in salmon pink.

4 (1^5/$_8$″)

a = 62 (24^3/$_8$″)
b = 77 (30^3/$_8$″)

Bind as instructed in (A) on page 3.

Piecing diagram

0.7cm (1/4″) seam allowance

Quilt with 2 strands of salmon pink embroidery floss.

5 3 5
b a b
c   c 5 (2″)
13 (5^1/$_8$″) a d a 3 (1^1/$_8$″)
c   c
b a b
13

Cutting

a: Cut 16 in salmon pink.
b: Cut 16 in polka dot.
c: Cut 16 in tartan.
d: Cut 4 in print.

Applique directions.

① Polka dot cotton

Batting

Place batting between top piece and applique piece, and blindstitch.

② Blindstitch

Print cotton

③ Baby cap

Wrong side Clip

Turn edges to wrong side, clip into fabric at curved edges and ease in fullness on curves with small running stitch.

④ Baby face

Embroider beforehand.

Synthetic filler

Baste baby cap in place, lay baby face on it and blindstitch, leaving an opening for stuffing with synthetic filler.

⑤ Lay thin synthetic filler, cover with applique piece and blindstitch.

綿

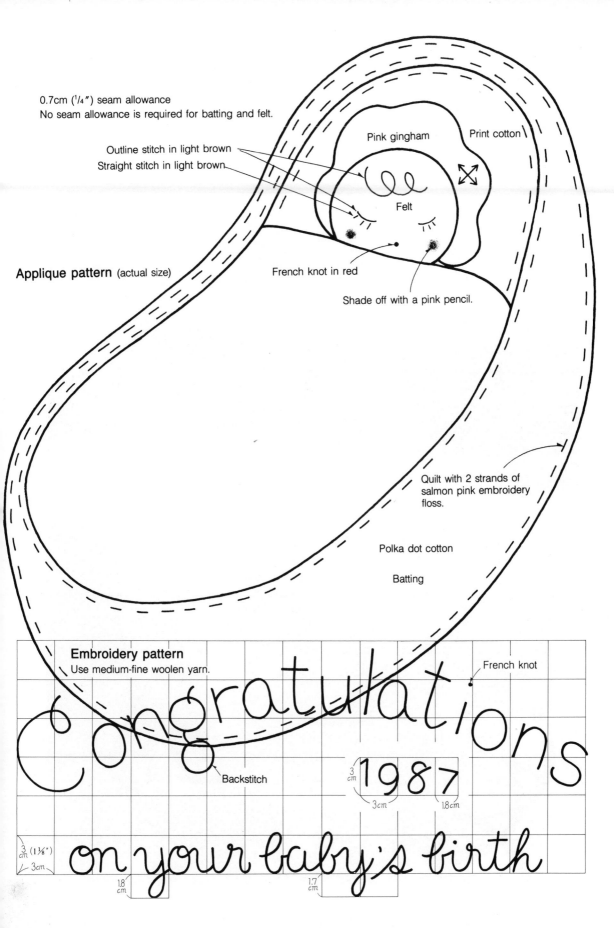

0.7cm (¹/₄″) seam allowance
No seam allowance is required for batting and felt.

Outline stitch in light brown
Straight stitch in light brown

Pink gingham

Print cotton

Felt

Applique pattern (actual size)

French knot in red

Shade off with a pink pencil.

Quilt with 2 strands of salmon pink embroidery floss.

Polka dot cotton

Batting

Embroidery pattern
Use medium-fine woolen yarn.

French knot

Congratulations

Backstitch

3 cm 1987 3cm 1.8cm

3 cm (1⅛″)
3cm

on your baby's birth

1.8 cm

1.7 cm

Crib Quilt directions on p.87

Crib Quilt directions on p.46

Hello, Sweet Baby

Crib Quilt p.45

Materials: 90cm by 60cm ($39^3/8'' \times 23^5/8''$) pink cotton, 90cm by 136cm ($39^3/8'' \times 53^1/2''$) light pink cotton, 90cm by 54cm ($39^3/8'' \times 21^1/4''$) white-and-pink print cotton, 90cm by 54cm ($39^3/8'' \times 21^1/4''$) white-and-pink checkered cotton, 90cm by 40cm ($39^3/8'' \times 15^3/4''$) white cotton. 1m by 130cm ($39^3/8'' \times 51^1/8''$) cotton for backing. 2 pieces of 112cm by 144cm ($44^7/8'' \times 56^3/4''$) synthetic filler. Embroidery floss: Small amount each of light pink, blue gray, pink and white.

Finished size: 104cm by 136cm ($41'' \times 53^1/2''$)

Directions: 1. Applique faces (*A* and *C*) and body (*D*) of rabbit with blindstitch to 18cm square of pink cotton (*b*). Join patch pieces (*b* and *c*) together after applique is finished. Applique face and forepaws of rabbit (*D*) with blindstitch to blocks.

2. Join patch pieces (*b* and *c*) together and applique rabbits (*B* and *E*). Embroider faces of rabbits (*A-E*).

3. Join patch pieces and blocks as shown in piecing diagram.

4. Place 2 pieces of synthetic filler between top piece and backing, baste all four together and finish right and left edges with binding (edges of synthetic filler are folded to be of four thickness as shown).

5. Finish top and bottom edges with binding similarly.

6. Quilt along crosswise seamlines.

1cm ($^3/8''$) seam allowance except for applique fabric.

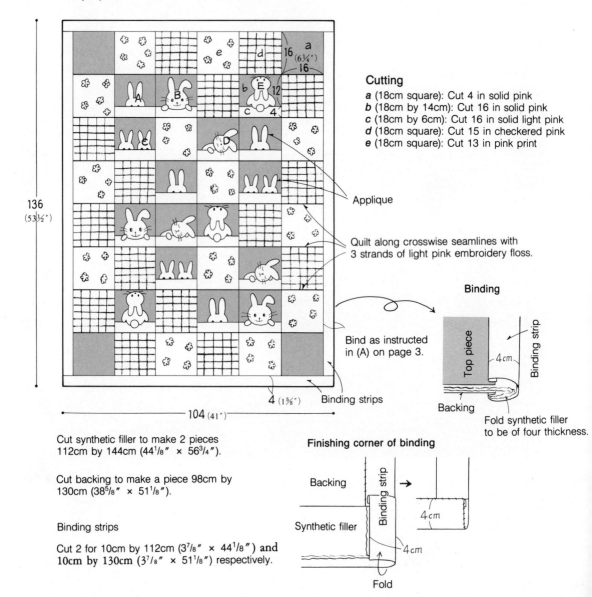

Cutting

a (18cm square): Cut 4 in solid pink
b (18cm by 14cm): Cut 16 in solid pink
c (18cm by 6cm): Cut 16 in solid light pink
d (18cm square): Cut 15 in checkered pink
e (18cm square): Cut 13 in pink print

Applique

Quilt along crosswise seamlines with 3 strands of light pink embroidery floss.

Binding

Bind as instructed in (A) on page 3.

Top piece
Binding strip
4cm
Backing
Fold synthetic filler to be of four thickness.

136 ($53^1/2''$)

104 ($41''$)

4 ($1^5/8''$) Binding strips

Cut synthetic filler to make 2 pieces 112cm by 144cm ($44^1/8'' \times 56^3/4''$).

Cut backing to make a piece 98cm by 130cm ($38^5/8'' \times 51^1/8''$).

Binding strips

Cut 2 for 10cm by 112cm ($3^7/8'' \times 44^1/8''$) and 10cm by 130cm ($3^7/8'' \times 51^1/8''$) respectively.

Finishing corner of binding

Backing
Binding strip
4cm
Synthetic filler
4cm
Fold

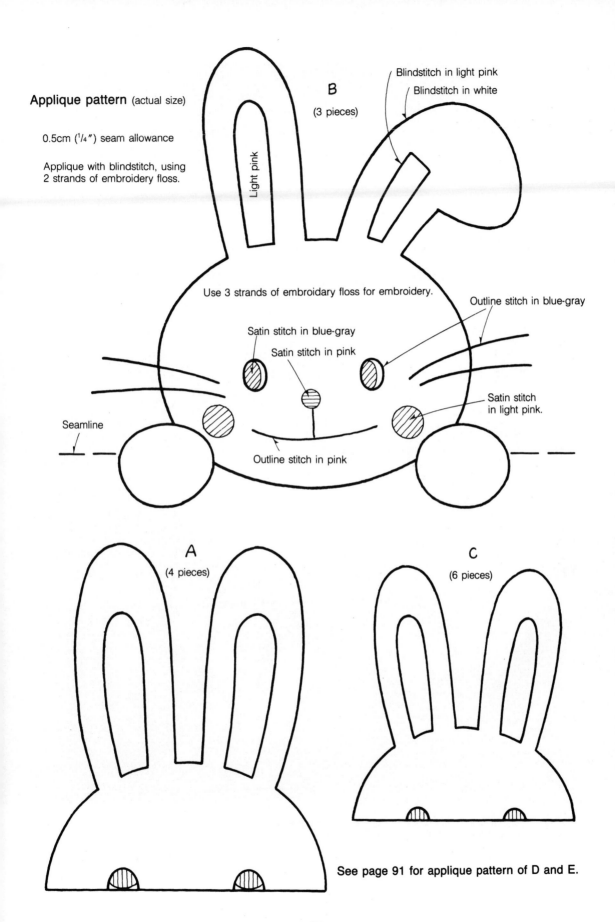

Applique pattern (actual size)

0.5cm (¹⁄₄″) seam allowance

Applique with blindstitch, using
2 strands of embroidery floss.

B
(3 pieces)

Light pink

Blindstitch in light pink
Blindstitch in white

Use 3 strands of embroidary floss for embroidery.

Satin stitch in blue-gray

Satin stitch in pink

Outline stitch in blue-gray

Satin stitch
in light pink.

Seamline

Outline stitch in pink

A
(4 pieces)

C
(6 pieces)

See page 91 for applique pattern of D and E.

In the Sunshine

Tea Cozy and Placemats directions on p.90

Lap Quilt p.48

Materials: Assorted cotton print scraps for *A-J* blocks. 90cm (35³/₈″) square of beige cotton. 4 pieces of 6.5cm (2¹/₂″) square cotton print for *b*. 84cm by 16cm (33¹/₁₆″ × 6¹/₄″) cotton print for *f*. 90cm by 16cm (35³/₈″ × 6¹/₄″) solid cotton for binding. 110cm (43¹/₄″) square backing. 110cm (43¹/₄″) square batting. Red and light brown 25-strand embroidery floss.

Seam allowance is 0.7cm (¹/₄″) except for binding strip.
Embroider after batting is placed between top piece and backing.

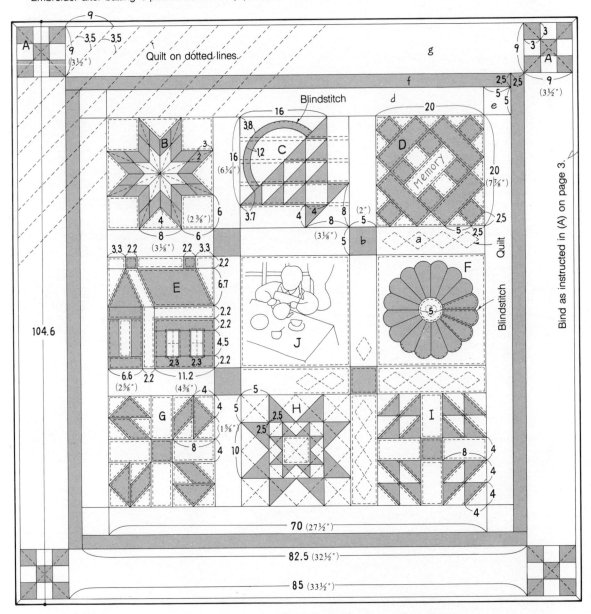

Cutting *a*: Cut 12 in beige.
　　　　d, *e* and *g*: Cut 4 of each in beige.
　　　　b and *f*: Cut 4 of each in print.

Cut backing and batting to make a piece
110cm (43¹/₄″) square respectively.

Binding strip
No seam allowance is required.

(1¼″) 3.2

422 (166⅛″)

Finished size: 105cm (41³/₈″) square
Directions: 1. Cut and join patch pieces to make A-I blocks.
2. Join the blocks (A-I) and patch pieces (J, a, b, d, e, f and g).

3. Lay top piece on batting, embroider it with D and J as shown. Lay top piece and batting on backing after embroidery is finished, and quilt as shown.
4. Finish edges wit binding.

Embroidery pattern (actual size)

Use 2 strands of red embroidery floss and embroider with outline stitch unless otherwise specified.

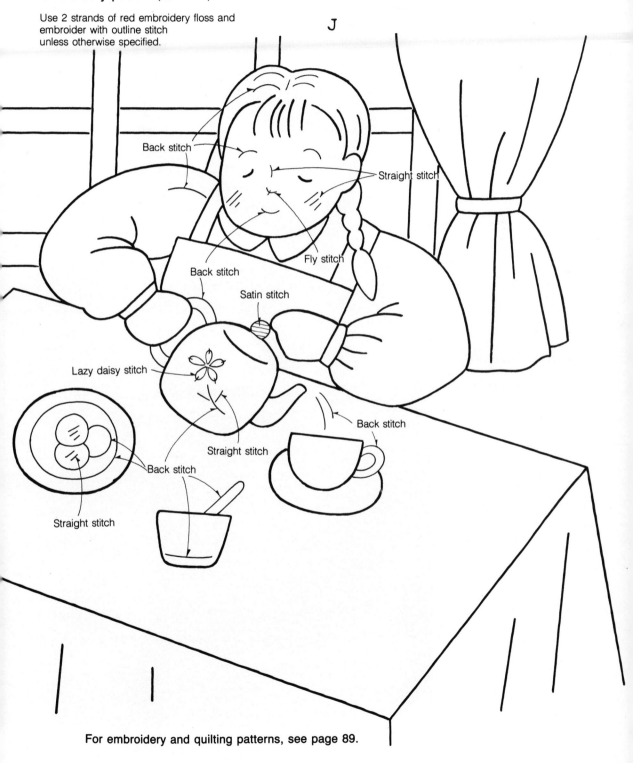

J

Back stitch

Straight stitch

Fly stitch

Back stitch

Satin stitch

Lazy daisy stitch

Back stitch

Straight stitch

Back stitch

Back stitch

Straight stitch

For embroidery and quilting patterns, see page 89.

In the Sunshine

Cutlery Basket directions on p.54

Table Napkin directions on p.55   **Tablecloth** directions on p.92

Cutlery Basket p.53

Materials: Assorted cotton scraps for patch pieces, border strips, loop and binding. 55cm by 30cm ($21^5/_8$" × $11^3/_4$") cotton for backing and inner liner. 78cm by 18cm ($30^3/_4$" × $7^7/_8$") thin batting. Brown embroidery floss. Medium-fine cotton cord. Rattan basket (26cm × 17cm × 8cm).

Directions: 1. Cut patch pieces, applique handle of flower basket with blindstitch as shown, and join patch pieces together to make 4 blocks.

2. Join 4 blocks and border strips (*A* and *B*) together.

3. Lay top piece on batting, embroider border strip (*B*) with letters and quilt.

4. Place two pieces of batting between top piece and backing, finish edges with binding and sew on a loop.

5. Hem edges of inner liner and seam its four corners as shown.

6. Lay inner liner into basket and sew on its corners to basket.

7. Sew on cotton cords to cover piece and tie them to basket.

For dimensions of block, see page 55.

0.7cm ($^1/_4$") seam allowance   **Basket cover**

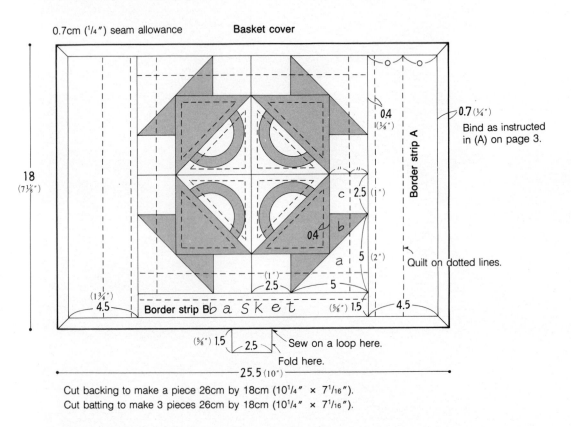

Bind as instructed in (A) on page 3.

Quilt on dotted lines.

Cut backing to make a piece 26cm by 18cm ($10^1/_4$" × $7^1/_{16}$").
Cut batting to make 3 pieces 26cm by 18cm ($10^1/_4$" × $7^1/_{16}$").

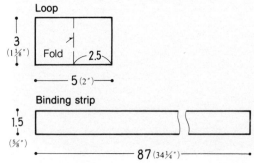

Loop

Embroidery pattern (actual size)

Backstitch with 2 strands

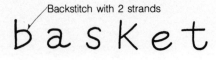

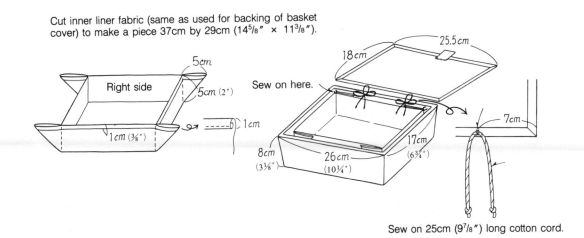

Cut inner liner fabric (same as used for backing of basket cover) to make a piece 37cm by 29cm ($14^5/_8'' \times 11^3/_8''$).

Sew on 25cm ($9^7/_8''$) long cotton cord.

Table Napkin p.52

Materials: 43cm ($16^7/_8''$) square cotton. Assorted cotton scraps for patch pieces.
Finished size: 40cm ($15^3/_4''$) square
Directions: 1. Cut patch pieces, applique handle of

flower basket pattern with blindstitch, and join patch pieces together as shown.
2. Applique pieced block with blindstitch to napkin foundation, quilt and hem edges.

1.5cm seam allowance

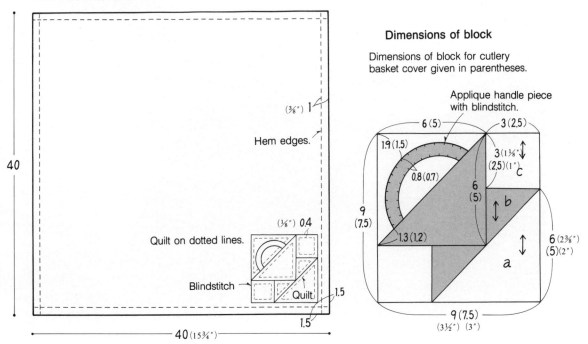

Cutlery Case directions on p.58   **Platemats** directions on p.94

In the Sunshine

Cutlery Case p.56

Materials: 90cm by 50cm (35³/₈″ × 19⁵/₈″) solid beige cotton. 24cm by 17cm (9¹/₂″ × 6³/₄″) print cotton. Assorted cotton scraps for patch pieces. 60cm by 23cm (23⁵/₈″ × 9″) batting. 30cm by 23cm (11³/₄″ × 9″) backing. Synthetic filler. Rose pink No. 25 embroidery floss. Light pink quilting thread.

Directions: 1. Cut and join patch pieces (*a*, *b*, *c* and *d*) together.

2. Place batting between top piece and backing, quilt and embroider as shown.

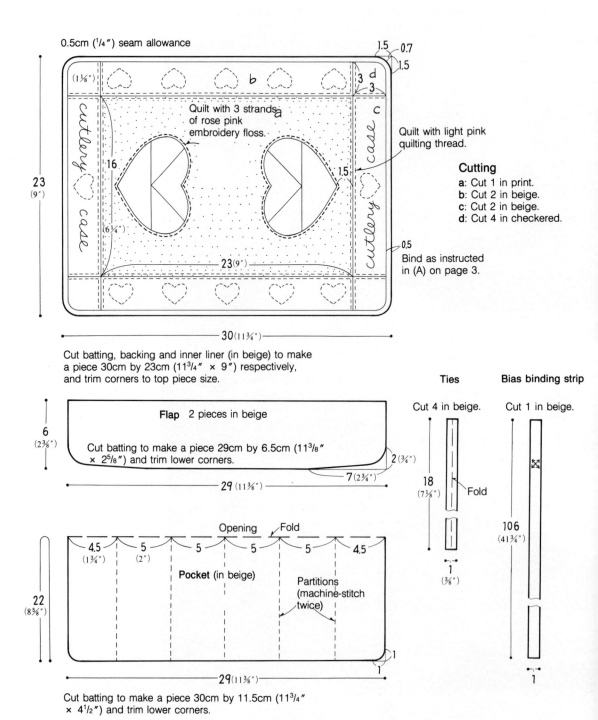

0.5cm (¹/₄″) seam allowance

Quilt with 3 strands of rose pink embroidery floss.

Quilt with light pink quilting thread.

Cutting
a: Cut 1 in print.
b: Cut 2 in beige.
c: Cut 2 in beige.
d: Cut 4 in checkered.

Bind as instructed in (A) on page 3.

Cut batting, backing and inner liner (in beige) to make a piece 30cm by 23cm (11³/₄″ × 9″) respectively, and trim corners to top piece size.

Flap 2 pieces in beige

Cut batting to make a piece 29cm by 6.5cm (11³/₈″ × 2⁵/₈″) and trim lower corners.

Ties
Cut 4 in beige.

Bias binding strip
Cut 1 in beige.

Opening Fold

Pocket (in beige)

Partitions (machine-stitch twice)

Cut batting to make a piece 30cm by 11.5cm (11³/₄″ × 4¹/₂″) and trim lower corners.

3. Cut and join patch pieces to make heart-shaped blocks. Applique blocks with blindstitch to top piece, stuffing with synthetic filler between. Quilt along edge of heart-shaped blocks.
4. Fold fabric for pocket in half, place batting between, lay it on inner liner, and stitch by machine to make partitions.
5. Lay top piece, inner liner and flap together, and finish edges with binding, setting ties in position as you blindstitch binding strips.

Flap

With right sides together, seam along raw edge, lay batting on it and turn right sides out.

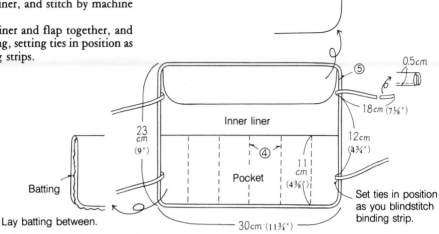

Heart-shaped pattern

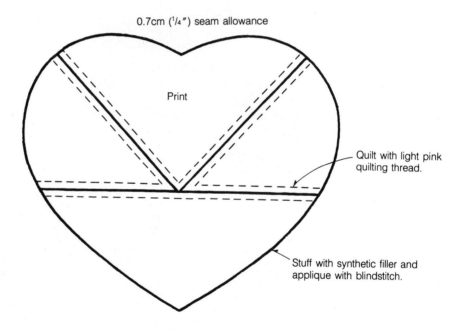

Embroidery and quilting patterns (actual size)

cutlery ♡ *case*

Backstitch with 3 strands of rose pink embroidery floss.

Quilt with light pink quilting thread.

In the Sunshine

Mitten directions on p.62

Pot Mats directions on p.93   **Potholders** directions on p.92

Mitten p.61

Materials: 56cm (22″) square wine-red cotton. 80cm by 8cm (31½″ × 3⅛″) unbleached muslin. 30cm by 8cm (11¾″ × 3⅛″) pink cotton. 30cm by 8cm (11¾″ × 3⅛″) white-and-red checkered cotton. 22cm by 28cm (8⅝″ × 3⅛″) unbleached prequilted cotton. 26cm by 32cm (10¼″ × 12⅝″) backing. 26cm by 32cm (10¼″ × 12⅝″) batting; Embroidery floss: Small amount each of off-white and pink.

Directions: 1. Cut and join patch pieces as shown. Place a template on pieced top, match marks and draw around it.

2. Place batting between top piece and backing, and quilt inside drawn lines.

3. Finish straight edge of front piece with binding strip A. Finish straight edge of back piece (prequilted cotton) with binding strip A.

4. With wrong sides of front and back pieces together, finish edge with binding strip B, trimming raw edges. Sew on a loop folded in half.

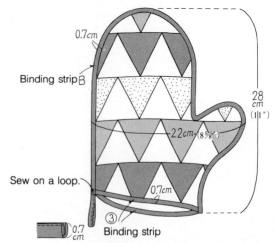

Finish both curved and straight edges with binding as instructed on page 3.

Loop

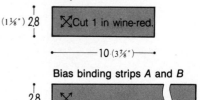

Cut 1 in wine-red.

(1⅛″) 2.8

10 (3⅞″)

Bias binding strips A and B

2.8

A = 16 (6¼″) Cut 2 in wine-red.
B = 73 (28¾″) Cut 1 in wine-red.

Front piece

Cut batting and backing to make a piece 26cm by 32cm (10¼″ × 12⅝″) respectively.

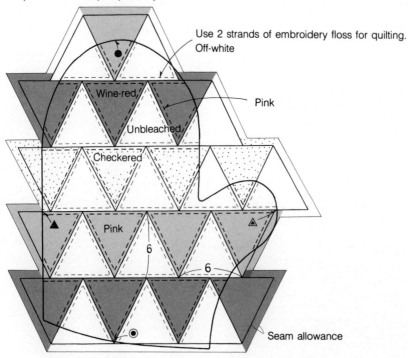

Use 2 strands of embroidery floss for quilting.
Off-white

Wine-red

Pink

Unbleached

Checkered

Pink

Pink

Seam allowance

62

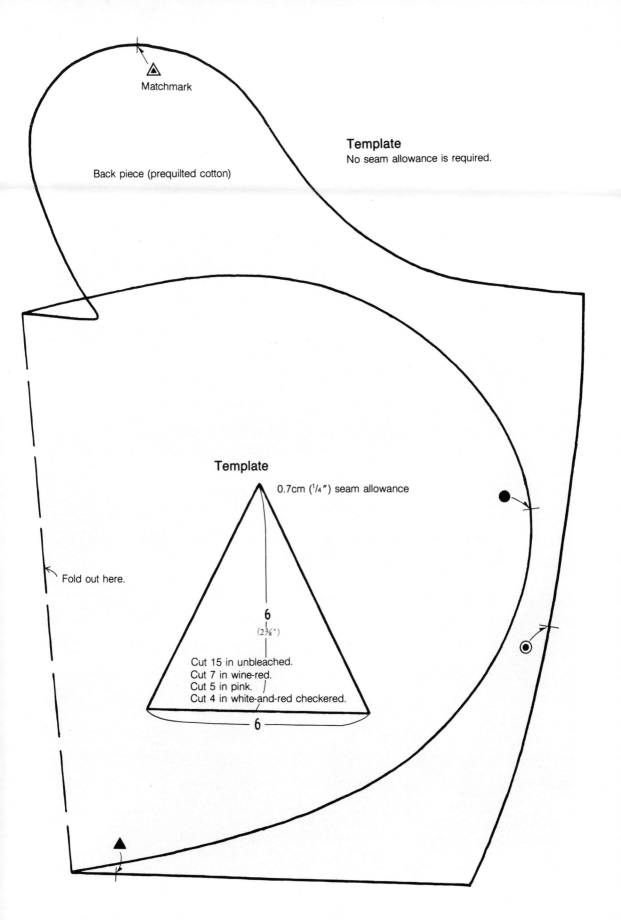

Matchmark

Back piece (prequilted cotton)

Template
No seam allowance is required.

Template

0.7cm (¹/₄″) seam allowance

Fold out here.

6
(2³/₈″)

Cut 15 in unbleached.
Cut 7 in wine-red.
Cut 5 in pink.
Cut 4 in white-and-red checkered.

6

Basket Cover directions on p.65

Basket Cover p.64

Materials: *a*: 90cm by 30cm (35³/₈″ × 11³/₄″) solid beige cotton. *b*: 24 patch pieces of 6.5cm (2¹/₂″) square medium print. *c*: 48 patch pieces of 4cm (1⁵/₈″) square dark print. *d*: 48 patch pieces of 4cm (1⁵/₈″) square light print. 60cm by 45cm (23⁵/₈″ × 17³/₄″) backing. 60cm by 45cm (23⁵/₈″ × 17³/₄″) thin batting. 90cm by 12cm (35³/₈″ × 4³/₃″) brown cotton for binding.

Finished size: 58cm by 44cm (23⁷/₈″ × 17³/₈″)
Directions: 1. Cut and join patch pieces (*a*, *b*, *c* and *d*).
2. Place batting between pieced top and backing, and quilt as shown.
3. Finish edges with binding.

0.7cm (¹/₄″) seam allowance except for binding strip.

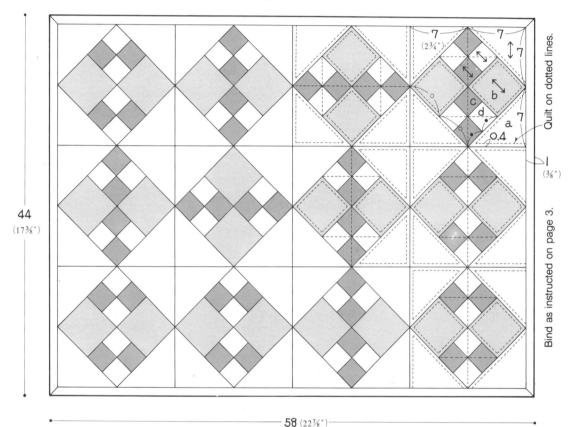

44 (17³/₈″)

Quilt on dotted lines.

Bind as instructed on page 3.

58 (22⁷/₈″)

Cut backing and batting to make a piece 60cm by 45cm (23⁵/₈″ × 17³/₄″) respectively.

No seam allowance is required.

(1⁵/₈″)4

Binding strip

206 (81¹/₈″)

Cutting
a: Cut 48 in beige.
b: Cut 24 in medium print.
c: Cut 48 in dark print.
d: Cut 48 in light print.

Basket Cover p.8

Materials: 90cm by 60cm ($35^3/8'' \times 23^5/8''$) unbleached muslin. 90cm by 60cm ($35^3/8'' \times 23^5/8''$) blue cotton print. 50cm ($19^5/8''$) square solid blue-gray cotton. 52cm ($20^1/2''$) square cotton for back piece. 50cm by 1m ($19^5/8'' \times 39^3/8''$) iron-on interfacing. 60cm by 112cm ($23^5/8'' \times 44^1/8''$) batting. 60cm by 112cm ($23^5/8'' \times 44^1/8''$) backing. 120cm of 3.6cm ($1^3/8''$) wide white satin ribbon. Medium-thick woolen yarn. Rattan basket (48cm ($47^1/4''$) in diameter, 35cm ($13^3/4''$) in height).

Finished size: 50cm ($19^5/8''$) in diameter

Directions: 1. Cut and join patch pieces (*a, b, c* and *d*) as shown.

2. Draw a circle of 50cm ($19^5/8''$) in diameter on pieced top. Place batting between top piece and backing, and quilt every 1.5cm ($5/8''$) inside drawn line as shown.

3. Draw a circle on back piece, place batting between back piece and backing, and quilt in the same way.

4. Put iron-on interfacing on backing of top and back pieces.

5. With wrong sides of top and back pieces together, lay binding strip on top piece and seam by machine. Trim raw edges to finished size.

6. Blindstitch binding strip to back piece, setting loops in position.

7. Sew on loops as shown. Put ribbon through loops and mesh of basket, and tie it.

Piecing diagram

0.7cm ($1/4''$) seam allowance

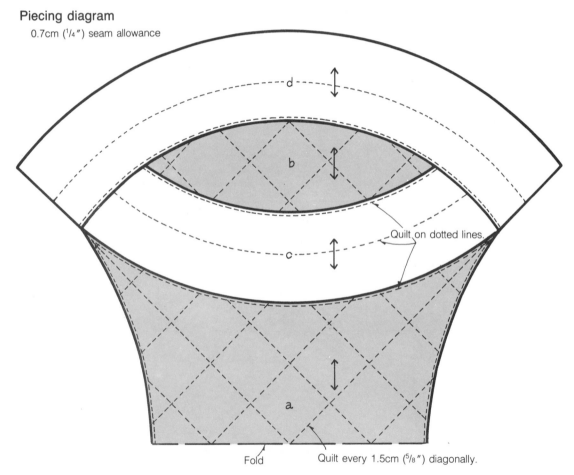

Quilt on dotted lines.

Fold

Quilt every 1.5cm ($5/8''$) diagonally.

Cutting

a: Cut 16 in blue print.
b: Cut 24 in blue print.
c: Cut 24 in unbleached.
d: Cut 24 in unbleached.

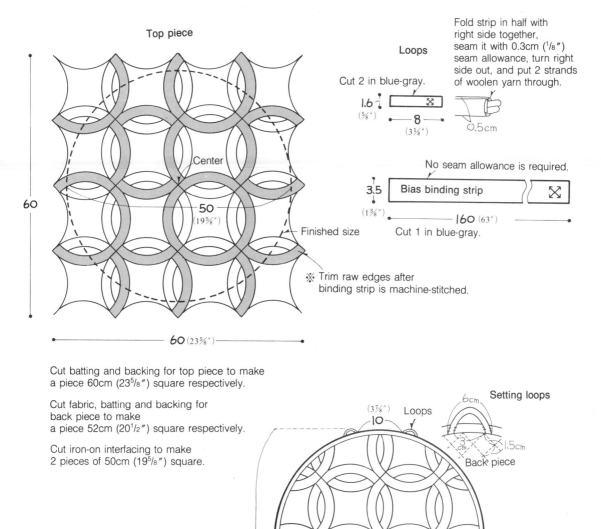

Top piece

Center

Finished size

50 (19⅝″)

60

60 (23⅝″)

Loops

Cut 2 in blue-gray.

Fold strip in half with right side together, seam it with 0.3cm (⅛″) seam allowance, turn right side out, and put 2 strands of woolen yarn through.

1.6 (⅝″)

8 (3⅛″)

0.5cm

No seam allowance is required.

3.5 (1⅜″)

Bias binding strip

160 (63″)

Cut 1 in blue-gray.

※ Trim raw edges after binding strip is machine-stitched.

Cut batting and backing for top piece to make a piece 60cm (23⅝″) square respectively.

Cut fabric, batting and backing for back piece to make a piece 52cm (20½″) square respectively.

Cut iron-on interfacing to make 2 pieces of 50cm (19⅝″) square.

Setting loops

Loops

6cm

(3⅞″) 10

3cm

1.5cm

Back piece

50 (19⅝″)

Bind as instructed on page 3.

Patchwork Picture p.17

Materials: Cotton scraps of 1 medium, 4 light and 4 dark prints. 60cm by 10cm (23⅝″ × 3⅞″) batting. 25cm by 17cm (9⅞″ × 6¾″) iron-on interfacing. Frame (See piecing diagram for inside dimensions.)

Directions: 1. Cut and join patch pieces to make 3 blocks of A and B respectively, and join blocks as shown.
2. Put iron-on interfacing on wrong side of top piece.
3. Trim raw edges to inside dimension of frame, and finish raw edges by machine stitch.

Piecing diagram and color scheme

▨ = Medium   ☐ = Light   ▓ = Dark

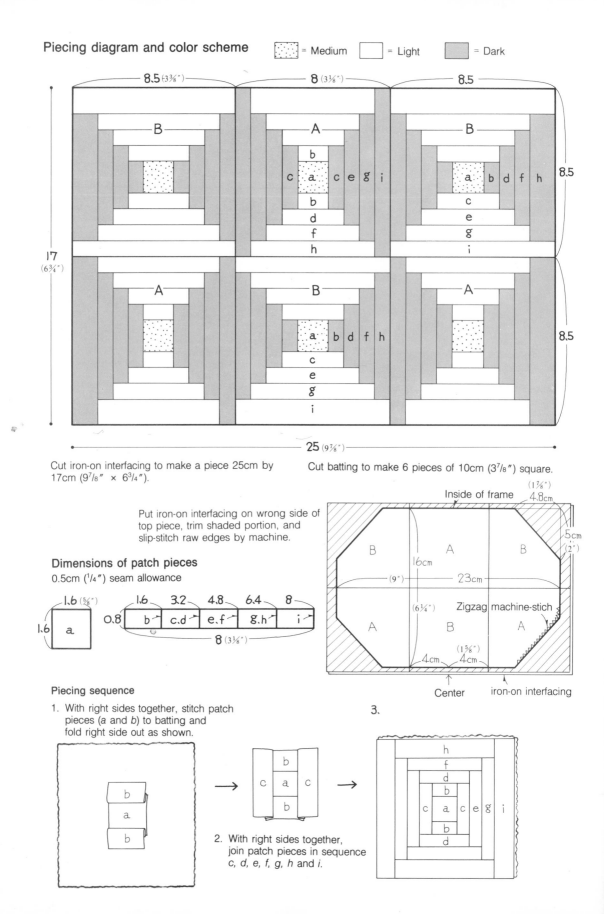

Cut iron-on interfacing to make a piece 25cm by 17cm (9⅞″ × 6¾″).

Cut batting to make 6 pieces of 10cm (3⅞″) square.

Put iron-on interfacing on wrong side of top piece, trim shaded portion, and slip-stitch raw edges by machine.

Dimensions of patch pieces

0.5cm (¼″) seam allowance

Piecing sequence

1. With right sides together, stitch patch pieces (a and b) to batting and fold right side out as shown.

2. With right sides together, join patch pieces in sequence c, d, e, f, g, h and i.

3.

Cushions A and B pp.12,13

Materials (for one cushion): *A:* 120cm by 35cm (47^1/$_4$″ × 13^3/$_4$″) charcoal-gray woolen; 88cm by 12cm (34^5/$_8$″ × 4^3/$_4$″) red checkered woolen; 48cm by 12cm (18^7/$_8$″ × 4^3/$_4$″) white checkered woolen; 47cm (18^1/$_2$″) square backing; Off-white embroidery floss; 38cm (15″) long zipper; Ready-made inner cushion of 40cm (15^3/$_4$″) square.

B: 120cm by 35cm (47^1/$_4$″ × 13^3/$_4$″) charcoal-gray woolen; 48cm by 12cm (18^7/$_8$″ × 4^3/$_4$″) red checkered woolen; 48cm by 12cm light brown checkered woolen; 48cm by 12cm white checkered woolen; 47cm (18^1/$_2$″) square backing; 38cm (15″) long zipper; Ready-made inner cushion of 40cm (15^3/$_4$″) square.

Finished size: 45cm (17^3/$_4$″) square
Directions: 1. Cut and join patch pieces, and join border strips to pieced top.
2. Join top piece and back pieces together, and sew on zipper.
3. With right sides of top piece and back piece together, place backing between and seam along edges. Turn right sides out.
4. Topstitch on seamline along border strip by machine.

Top piece for *A*

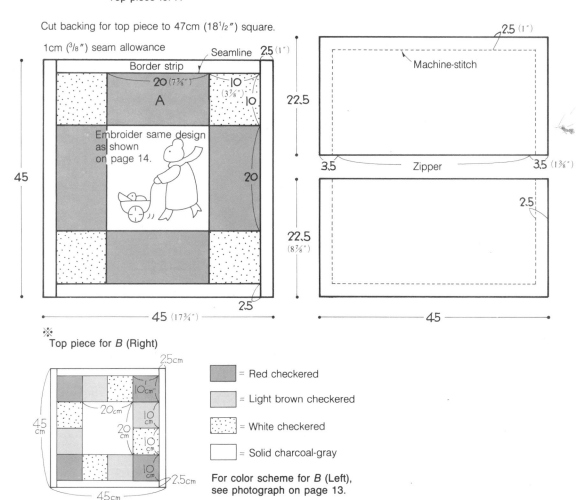

For color scheme for *B* (Left),
see photograph on page 13.

69

Wall Hanging p.25

Materials: 90cm by 150cm (35³/₈″ × 59¹/₂″) solid red cotton. 60cm by 20cm (23⁵/₈″ × 7⁷/₈″) white cotton. Assorted dark and light red print scraps. Assorted unbleached dark and light print scraps. 100cm by 70cm (27¹/₂″ × 17³/₄″) batting. 83cm by 47cm (32⁵/₈″ × 18¹/₂″) batting. White embroidery floss. Red and white quilting thread.

Finished size: 45cm by 80.5cm (17³/₄″ × 31³/₄″)

Directions: 1. For pockets *A* and *C*, cut and join patch pieces together. For pocket *B*, cut and join patch pieces to make heart-shaped block, applique pieced block to pocket foundation, and embroider.

2. Lay top piece for pocket on batting and quilt. With right sides of top piece and backing together, seam along upper edge and turn right sides out.

3. Seam lower edge of pocket pieces (*A* and *B*) to foundation fabric, and baste pocket piece (*C*) to foundation fabric.

4. Join border strips to foundation.

5. Lay top piece on batting layers, topstitch for partition of pocket (*A*) and quilt as shown.

6. Baste loops in position to foundation. With right sides of top piece and backing together, seam along edges, leaving small opening for turning. Turn right sides out and seam opening with overcasting-stitch.

1cm (³/₈″) seam allowance

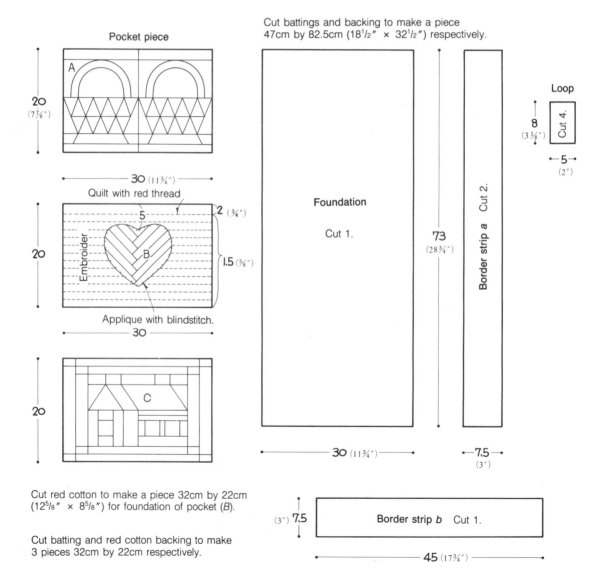

Cut red cotton to make a piece 32cm by 22cm (12⁵/₈″ × 8⁵/₈″) for foundation of pocket (*B*).

Cut batting and red cotton backing to make 3 pieces 32cm by 22cm respectively.

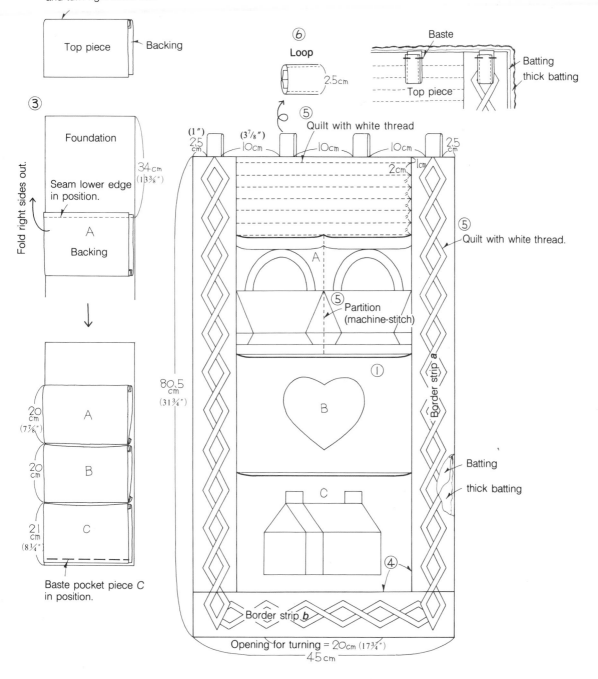

② With right sides together, seam along upper edge and turn right sides out.

Top piece — Backing

⑥
Loop
2.5cm

Baste
Batting
thick batting
Top piece

③
Foundation

Seam lower edge in position.

Fold right sides out.

34cm
(13⅜")

A
Backing

(1")
2.5cm
(3⅞")
10cm
10cm
10cm
2.5cm

⑤ Quilt with white thread

2cm
1cm

A

⑤ Quilt with white thread.

⑤ Partition (machine-stitch)

Border strip a

①

80.5cm
(31¾")

B

Batting
thick batting

20cm
(7⅞")
A

20cm
B

21cm
(8¼")
C

C

④

Baste pocket piece C in position.

Border strip b

Opening for turning = 20cm (17¾")
45cm

Piecing diagram of each block

0.7cm (¼″) seam allowance

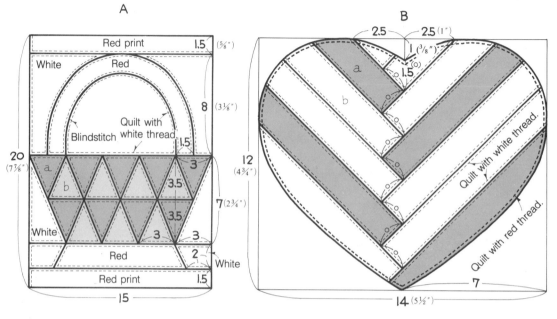

A

Red print — 1.5 (⅝″)

White — Red

8 (3⅛″)

Blindstitch — Quilt with white thread

1.5

20 (7⅞″)

a — b — 3

3.5

3.5

White — 3 — 3

Red — 2 — White

Red print — 1.5

15

a in dark print   *b* in light print

B

2.5 — 2.5 (1″)

1 (⅜″)

a — 1.5

b

12 (4¾″)

Quilt with white thread.

Quilt with red thread.

7

14 (5½″)

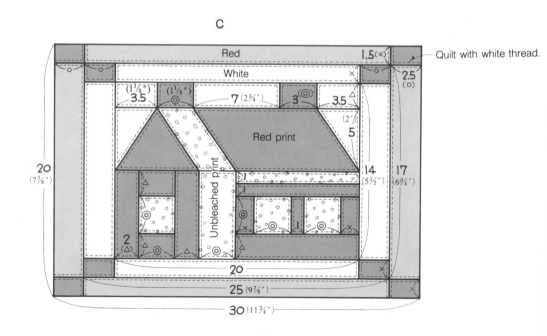

C

Red — 1.5 (×) — Quilt with white thread.

White — 2.5 (○)

(1⅜″) 3.5 — (1⅛″) — 7 (2¾″) — 3 (◎) — 3.5

(2″) 5

Red print

14 (5½″)

17 (6¾″)

20 (7⅞″)

Unbleached print

2 (△)

20

25 (9⅞″)

30 (11¾″)

72

Function has always existed side-by-side with the products of fashionable taste. Design and can be seen in "fork" objects and tools the world over of all ages.

Embroidery pattern (actual size)

Use 2 strands of white embroidery floss and outline stitch.

Quilting pattern (actual size)

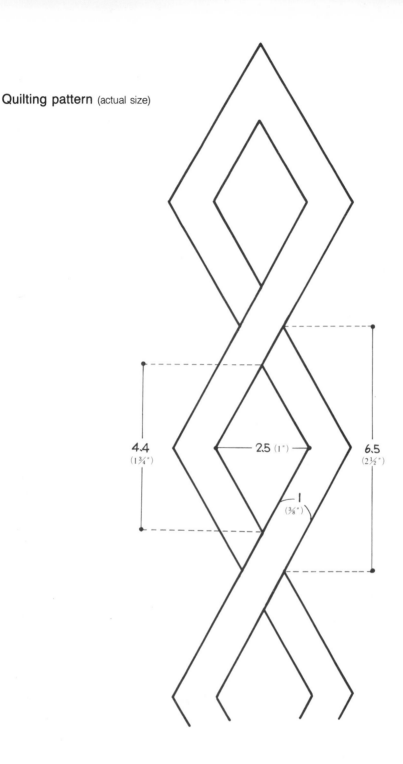

4.4
(1¾")

2.5 (1")

6.5
(2½")

1
(⅜")

Continued from p.27

Directions: 1. *Miniature quilt A*: Cut and join assorted brown print patch pieces, lay pieced top on wrong side of 8cm by 12cm (3¹/₈″ × 4³/₄″) polka dot backing, bind edges with backing, and quilt.

2. *Miniature quilt B*: Cut and join assorted blue print patch pieces, lay pieced top on wrong side of 11cm

(4³/₈″) square blue backing, bind edges with backing, and quilt.

3. Applique miniature quilts (*A* and *B*) and rod to wall.

4. Applique table to wall, and fabrics, bear and flag to table, then embroider.

Shopwindow A (actual size)

Cut applique pieces, adding 0.5cm (¹/₄″) seam allowance, and blindstitch.
Use 2 strands of floss for embroidery.

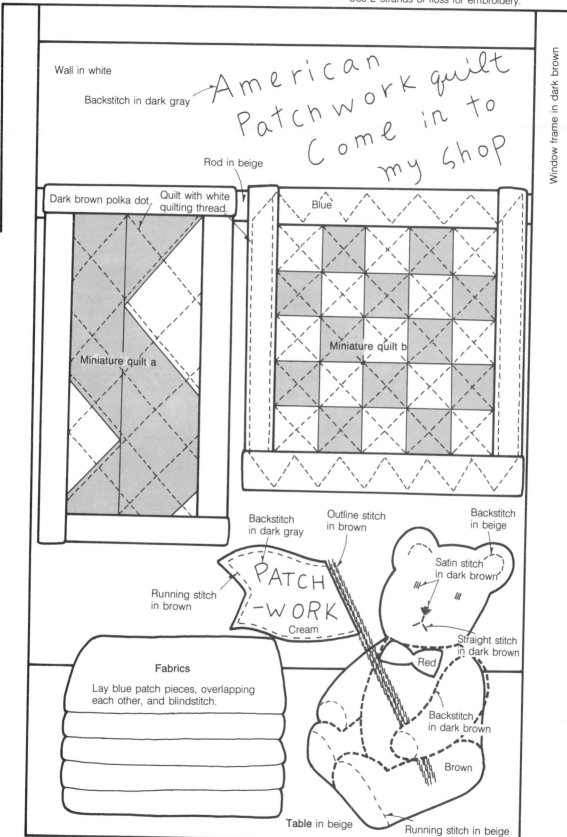

Wall in white

Backstitch in dark gray

American Patchwork quilt Come in to my shop

Window frame in dark brown

Rod in beige

Dark brown polka dot

Quilt with white quilting thread.

Blue

Miniature quilt a

Miniature quilt b

Backstitch in dark gray

Outline stitch in brown

Backstitch in beige

Satin stitch in dark brown

Running stitch in brown

PATCH -WORK

Cream

Straight stitch in dark brown

Red

Fabrics

Lay blue patch pieces, overlapping each other, and blindstitch.

Backstitch in dark brown

Brown

Table in beige

Running stitch in beige

Signboard (actual size)

Add 0.5cm (1/4") seam allowance, and blindstitch.

Unbleached white

HAND MADE QUILT SHOP

Blue

Running stitch with
white quilting thread

Backstitch in
3 strands dark pink

Backstitch in
3 strands dark brown

Blue

Running stitch
in 3 strands blue

Use No. 25 embroidery floss except specified.

Applique of signboard

Directions: 1. Cut applique pieces in unbleached
white and blue.
2. Embroider letters, stems and leaves as shown.
3. Turn edges to back and topstitch with running
stitch.
4. Applique signboard to roof.
5. Blindstitch blue applique pieces through roof piece.

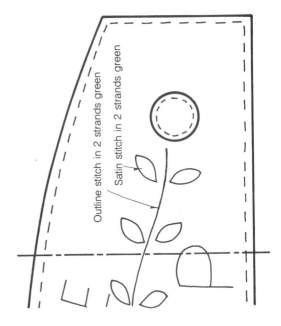

Outline stitch in 2 strands green

Satin stitch in 2 strands green

Applique of shopwindow B

Directions: 1. Miniature quilt: Cut basket pieces in
flower print and applique them to cherry-pink foundation. Lay top piece on wrong side of 15cm by 18cm
(5⁷/₈" × 7¹/₁₆") checkered backing, bind edges
with backing, and embroider letters.
2. Applique miniature quilt to wall, and embroider
hanging rope.
3. Applique table to wall.
4. Bag *a*: Cut and join patch pieces, applique pieced
top to unbleached white piece, and embroider as
shown.
5. Bag *b*: Cut and join 4 assorted patch pieces, and
finish upper edge with binding.
6. Bag *c*: Applique flower print square to yellow foundation, turn under upper edge and topstitch with
running stitch, then embroider as shown.
7. Make handles and sew on each to wrong side of
upper end of bag piece.
8. Applique bags to table, leaving upper end open.

Shopwindow B (actual size)

Outline stitch in dark gray

Cut applique pieces, adding 0.5cm (¼″) seam allowance, and blindstitch.
Use 2 strands of floss for embroidery.

Wall in white

Window frame in dark brown

Binding in checkered

Foundation in cherry-pink

Flower print

Have a good time.

Backstitch in white

Bag

Binding

Running olive-green

Unbleached white

Satin dark blue

Running dark blue

Satin white

Dark blue

a

b

Green print

Quilt with white thread.

c

KUMI

Flower print

Yellow

Straight olive-green

Table in beige

Quilting pattern (actual size)

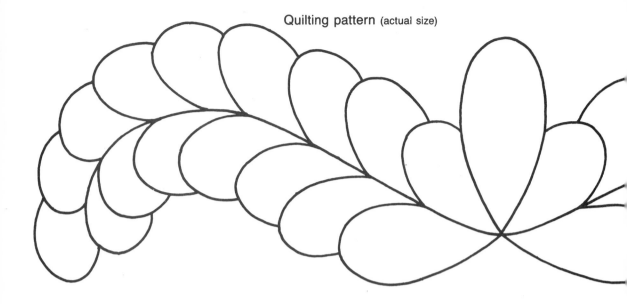

Continued from p.19

Directions: 1. Cut patch pieces for top and backing, sew stuff and join together as shown. Join pieced top to border strips with blindstitch.

2. Sew on zipper to back piece.
3. With right sides of front and back pieces together, stitch along raw edges and turn right sides out.

0.5cm (¼″) seam allowance

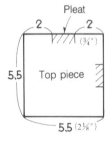

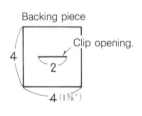

Cutting

Top piece: D: Cut 25 in blue-gray.
E. Cut 21 in light brown.
E. Cut 4 in olive-green.

Backing piece: D: Cut 25 in blue-gray.
E. Cut 25 in brown.

1

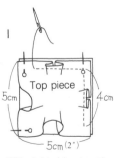

With right sides together, pin top piece to backing piece, make pleats in center of four sides of top piece, and stitch.

2

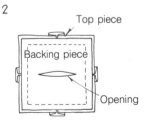

Turn right sides out.

3

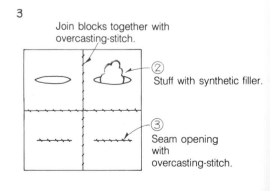

Join blocks together with overcasting-stitch.

② Stuff with synthetic filler.

③ Seam opening with overcasting-stitch.

Front piece

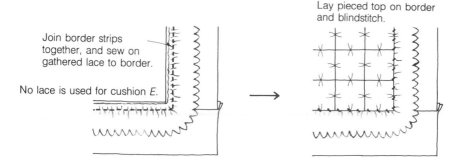

Join border strips together, and sew on gathered lace to border.

No lace is used for cushion *E*.

Lay pieced top on border and blindstitch.

Lampshade p.29

Materials: 80cm by 7cm ($31^1/_2" \times 2^3/_4"$) light reddish brown cotton. 80cm by 7cm dark red cotton. 80cm by 7cm coral-pink print cotton. 80cm by 11cm ($31^1/_2" \times 4^3/_8"$) dark purple print cotton. 80cm by 11cm rose-pink print cotton. 74cm by 24cm ($29^1/_8"$ $\times$ $9^1/_2"$) backing. 1m ($39^3/_8"$) of 1cm ($^3/_8"$) wide rose-pink cotton tape. Lamp stand and shade frame kit (frame: 20cm ($7^7/_8"$) high and 23cm ($9"$) in bottom diameter).

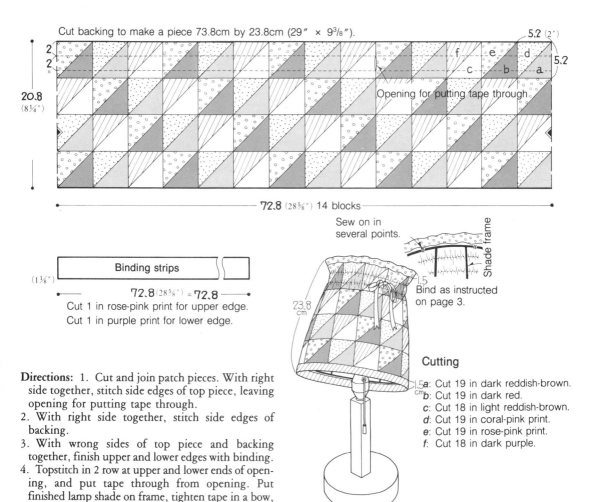

Cut backing to make a piece 73.8cm by 23.8cm ($29" \times 9^3/_8"$).

5.2 ($2"$)

2
2

20.8
($8^1/_4"$)

f e d
c b a

5.2

Opening for putting tape through

72.8 ($28^5/_8"$) 14 blocks

Binding strips

($1^1/_8"$)

72.8 ($28^5/_8"$) = 72.8

Cut 1 in rose-pink print for upper edge.
Cut 1 in purple print for lower edge.

Sew on in several points.

Shade frame

1.5

Bind as instructed on page 3.

23.8 cm

Cutting

1.5 cm

a: Cut 19 in dark reddish-brown.
b: Cut 19 in dark red.
c: Cut 18 in light reddish-brown.
d: Cut 19 in coral-pink print.
e: Cut 19 in rose-pink print.
f: Cut 18 in dark purple.

Directions: 1. Cut and join patch pieces. With right side together, stitch side edges of top piece, leaving opening for putting tape through.
2. With right side together, stitch side edges of backing.
3. With wrong sides of top piece and backing together, finish upper and lower edges with binding.
4. Topstitch in 2 row at upper and lower ends of opening, and put tape through from opening. Put finished lamp shade on frame, tighten tape in a bow, and sew on shade to frame at several points.

Pincushions pp.32,33

Materials (for 1 pincushion): 60cm by 40cm ($23^5/8''$ × $15^3/4''$) print cotton. Extra thick woolen yarn. Synthetic filler. 30cm ($11^3/4''$) ribbon (Left: Tie 2 strips of ribbon together in a bow.)

Directions: Cut and join bias strips for basket and handle and make tubes as shown. Form basket with tube, starting from bottom and working around bottom like a coil, keeping seam on inside, as shown. Sew in place with slipstitch. Sew handle tube in place as shown. With right sides together, seam top and back pieces for pincushion, leaving an opening for turning. Turn right sides out, stuff with synthetic filler and seam opening with slipstitch. Put pincushion into basket.

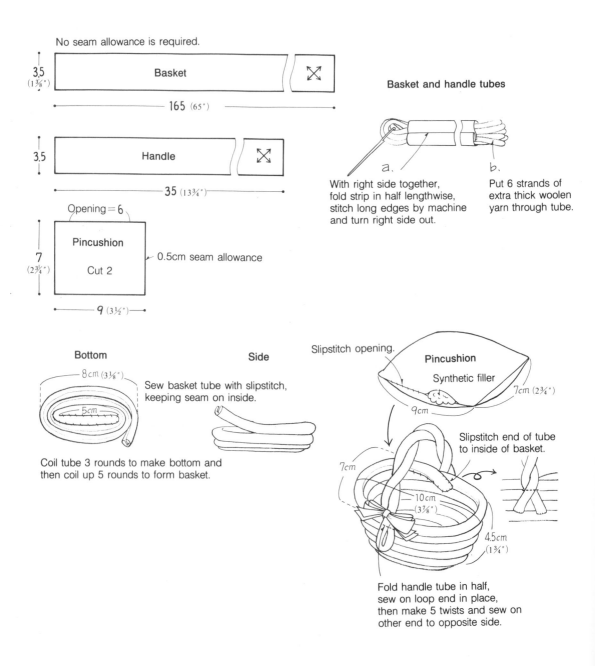

No seam allowance is required.

Basket

3,5 ($1^3/8''$)

165 (65")

Basket and handle tubes

Handle

3,5

35 ($13^3/4''$)

a.
With right side together, fold strip in half lengthwise, stitch long edges by machine and turn right side out.

b.
Put 6 strands of extra thick woolen yarn through tube.

Opening = 6

Pincushion

Cut 2

0.5cm seam allowance

7 ($2^3/4''$)

9 ($3^1/2''$)

Bottom

8cm ($3^1/8''$)

5cm

Coil tube 3 rounds to make bottom and then coil up 5 rounds to form basket.

Side

Sew basket tube with slipstitch, keeping seam on inside.

Slipstitch opening.

Pincushion
Synthetic filler

7cm ($2^3/4''$)

9cm

Slipstitch end of tube to inside of basket.

7cm

10cm ($3^7/8''$)

4.5cm ($1^3/4''$)

Fold handle tube in half, sew on loop end in place, then make 5 twists and sew on other end to opposite side.

Bag A p.36

Materials: *Bag:* 90cm by 35cm (35³/₈″ × 13³/₄″) beige cotton, 90cm by 6cm (35³/₈″ × 2³/₈″) beige print cotton. 63cm by 31cm (24³/₄″ × 12¹/₈″) backing. 61cm by 37cm (24″ × 14⁵/₈″) batting. *Mascot doll:* 13cm by 8.5cm (5¹/₈″ × 3³/₈″) black cotton, 13cm by 4.5cm (5¹/₈″ × 1³/₄″) print cotton. 13cm (5¹/₈″) of 1.5cm wide cream-colored tulle lace. Black cotton thread. Embroidery floss: Small amount each of white and red. 1 pearl-bead of 0.3cm (¹/₈″) in diameter. 12cm (4³/₄″) of 0.4cm (¹/₈″) wide satin ribbon. Synthetic filler.

Directions: 1. Cut and join patch pieces. Join pieced strip to upper and lower strips.

2. Place batting between top piece and backing, and quilt as shown.
3. With right side together, seam side edges of outer piece, and bind seamed edges with backing and topstitch as shown.
4. Lay top piece for bottom on batting, quilt and turn in seam allowance. Stitch along lower edge of outer piece and gather. Seam top piece of bottom to gathered end by machine.
5. Turn in seam allowance of bottom backing, and slipstitch it to wrong side of outer piece.
6. Finish upper edge of outer piece with binding.
7. Sew on handle in place by machine, and sew the mascot doll on by hand.

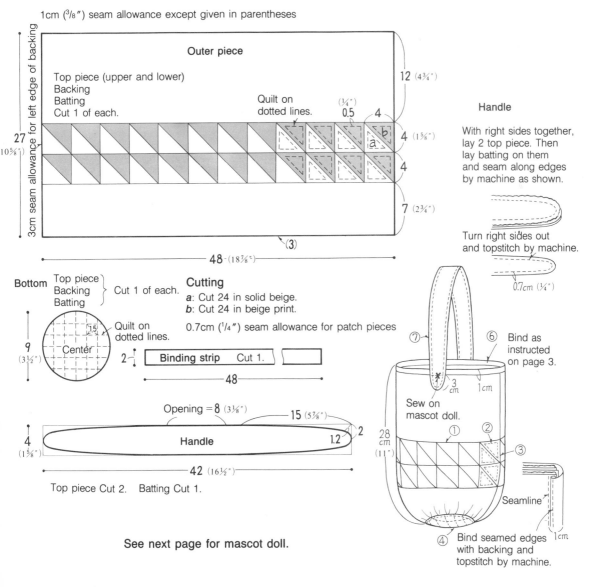

See next page for mascot doll.

Mascot doll

Directions: 1. Cut doll pieces. With right sides together, seam pieces, leaving an opening for turning. Turn right sides out, stuff with synthetic filler and seam opening with slipstitch.
2. Cut dress piece in print. With right side together, seam edges, leaving opening for armhole, and seam lace to lower edge.
3. Slipstitch upper end of armhole opening to shoulder length. Stitch upper edge of dress piece and gather. Put it on doll body and sew on at neck.
4. Embroider doll face, sew on hair as shown, and set a bow with bead.

Pattern

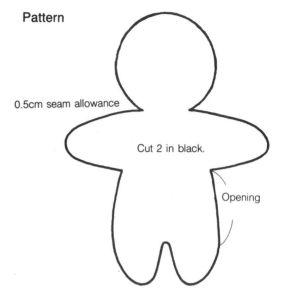

0.5cm seam allowance

Cut 2 in black.

Opening

0.5cm (¹/₄″) seam allowance

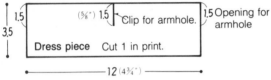

1.5   (⅝″) 1.5   Clip for armhole.   1.5 Opening for armhole

3.5

Dress piece   Cut 1 in print.

12 (4¾″)

Running stitch along upper edge

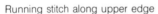

0.5cm

Slipstitch to shoulder length

Lace   0.7cm

4 strands of black cotton thread

1.2 cm (⅝″)

Tie here.

Tie 12cm (4¾″) ribbon in a bow, and set it with pearl-bead.

Satin stitch in 2 strands white

Backstitch in 2 strands red

7 cm (2¾″)

Bow

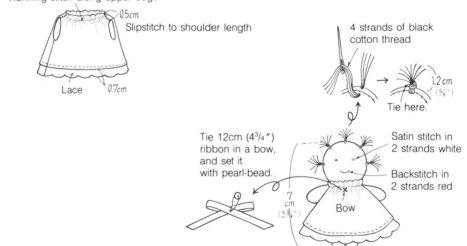

82

Bag B p.37

Materials: *Bag:* 90cm by 22cm (35³/₈″ × 8⁵/₈″) black cotton, 63cm by 21cm (24³/₄″ × 8¹/₄″) striped print cotton, 65cm by 31cm (25⁵/₈″ × 12¹/₂″) backing, 63cm by 37cm (24³/₄″ × 14⁵/₈″) batting, 1 ring of 2.7cm (1″) in inner diameter, 12cm (4³/₄″) of 1cm (³/₈″) wide black satin ribbon.
Mascot doll: Same materials used for mascot doll for Bag *A* (See page 81.)
Directions: 1. Cut and join black and striped strips.
2. Place batting between top piece and backing, and quilt on stripe lines.
3. With right side together, seam side edges of outer

piece, and bind seamed edges with backing and top-stitch as shown.
4. Lay top piece for bottom on batting, quilt and turn in seam allowance. Stitch along lower edge of outer piece and gather. Seam top piece of bottom to gathered end by machine.
5. Turn in seam allowance of bottom backing and seam it to wrong side of outer piece with slipstitch.
6. Finish upper edge with binding.
7. Sew on handle in place. Put satin ribbon through ring, and sew on ribbon together with one end of handle.
8. Sew on mascot doll in place (see page 82.).

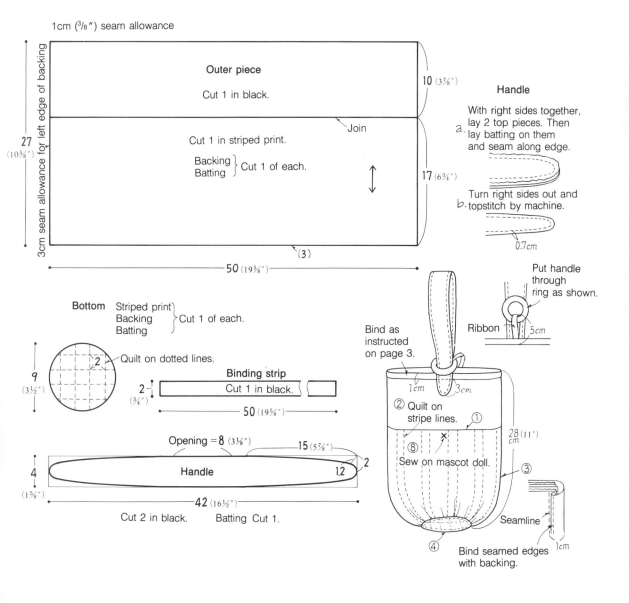

Bag C pp.36,37

Materials: 75cm by 50cm ($29^{1}/_{2}''$ × $19^{5}/_{8}''$) beige cotton. 3 assorted print cotton scraps for patch pieces. 45cm by 26cm ($17^{3}/_{4}''$ × $10^{1}/_{4}''$) backing. 43cm by 27cm ($16^{7}/_{8}''$ × $10^{5}/_{8}''$) batting. 1m ($39^{3}/_{8}''$) of beige waxed cotton rope (0.3cm in diameter). Extrathick woolen yarn.

Directions: 1. Cut and join patch pieces, and applique pieced block to top piece with blindstitch. Place batting between top piece and backing, and quilt as shown.

2. Place batting between top piece and backing for bottom, and quilt.

3. With right side together, seam along side edges of outer piece, and bind seamed edges with backing and topstitch as shown.

4. With right sides together, seam outer piece and bottom piece, and bind seamed edges with backing of outer piece.

5. Fold lapel inside and slipstitch it to backing. Stitch strips for strap on outer piece as shown.

6. Make handle tube and sew on its ends inside.

7. Put cotton rope through straps and finish ends of rope with decorative print scrap as shown.

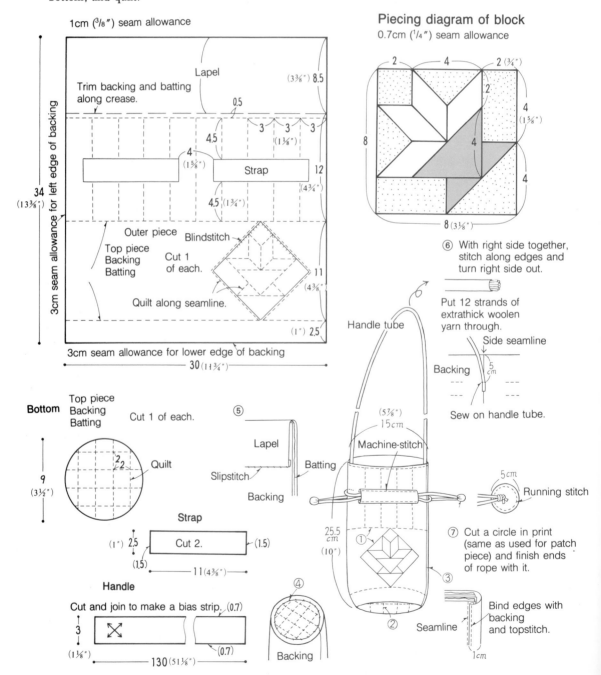

1cm ($^{3}/_{8}''$) seam allowance

Lapel

Trim backing and batting along crease.

($3^{3}/_{8}''$) 8.5

0.5

3   3   3

4.5   ($1^{1}/_{8}''$)

4 ($1^{5}/_{8}''$)

Strap

12 ($4^{3}/_{4}''$)

4.5 ($1^{3}/_{4}''$)

Outer piece   Blindstitch

Top piece   Cut 1
Backing   of each.
Batting

11 ($4^{3}/_{8}''$)

Quilt along seamline.

(1") 2.5

3cm seam allowance for left edge of backing

34 ($13^{3}/_{8}''$)

3cm seam allowance for lower edge of backing

30 ($11^{3}/_{4}''$)

Piecing diagram of block

0.7cm ($^{1}/_{4}''$) seam allowance

2   4   2 ($^{3}/_{4}''$)

2

4 ($1^{5}/_{8}''$)

8   4

4

4

8 ($3^{1}/_{8}''$)

⑥ With right side together, stitch along edges and turn right side out.

Put 12 strands of extrathick woolen yarn through.

Side seamline

Backing   5 cm

Sew on handle tube.

Bottom Top piece
Backing   Cut 1 of each.
Batting

9 ($3^{1}/_{2}''$)

2   2   Quilt

⑤

Lapel

Slipstitch   Batting

Backing

Strap

(1") 2.5   Cut 2.   (1.5)

(1.5)

11 ($4^{3}/_{8}''$)

Handle

Cut and join to make a bias strip. (0.7)

3 ($1^{1}/_{8}''$)

(0.7)

130 ($51^{1}/_{8}''$)

Handle tube

($5^{7}/_{8}''$) 15cm

Machine-stitch

5cm

Running stitch

25.5 cm

(10")   ①

②   Seamline

③

④

Backing

⑦ Cut a circle in print (same as used for patch piece) and finish ends of rope with it.

Bind edges with backing and topstitch.

1cm

Photo Album Cover p.41

Materials: *Top:* 87cm by 37cm (34¼″ × 14⅝″) unbleached cotton, 21cm by 11cm (8½″ × 4⅜″) blue polka dot cotton, solid and print cotton scraps. 25cm (9⅞″) square batting coral-pink medium-thick woolen yarn. Vermilion embroidery floss.
Bottom: 87cm by 37cm (34¼″ × 14⅝″) un-

bleached cotton, print cotton scraps. 20cm (7⅞″) square batting. Red medium-thick woolen yarn.
Finished size: 29cm by 38cm (11⅜″ × 15″)
Directions: Applique and embroider as shown. You may have albums made by custom album maker, using finished top piece.

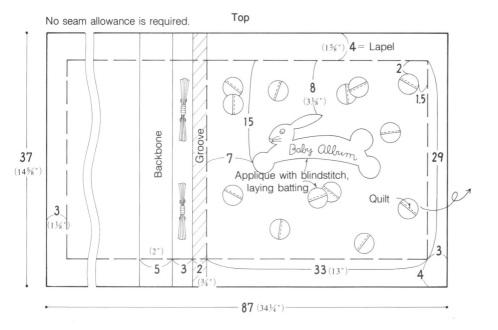

No seam allowance is required.

Top

(1⅝″) **4** = Lapel

Backbone

Groove

15

7

Applique with blindstitch, laying batting

8 (3⅛″)

2
1.5

29

Quilt

1

3

3 (1⅛″)

(2″)

5 3 2 (¾″)

33 (13″)

37 (14⅝″)

4

87 (34¼″)

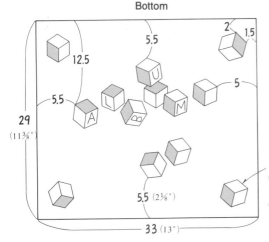

Bottom

2 1.5
5.5
12.5
5.5
5
5.5
A
L
U
M
5.5 (2⅛″)
33 (13″)
29 (11⅜″)

Cut 1 in dark and 2 in light for 1 block to make it look like a cubic.

Applique of cirlces:

1. Cut half circles, and seam straight edges, with right sides together. Press seam allowance and topstitch.
2. Stitch around edge with running stitch, lay paper pattern on wrong side and ease in fullness on curves and iron, then remove pattern.

pattern

3. Applique with blindstitch, laying batting between.
Batting

Cut and join 3 patch pieces, and applique pieced blocks with blindstitch, laying batting between.

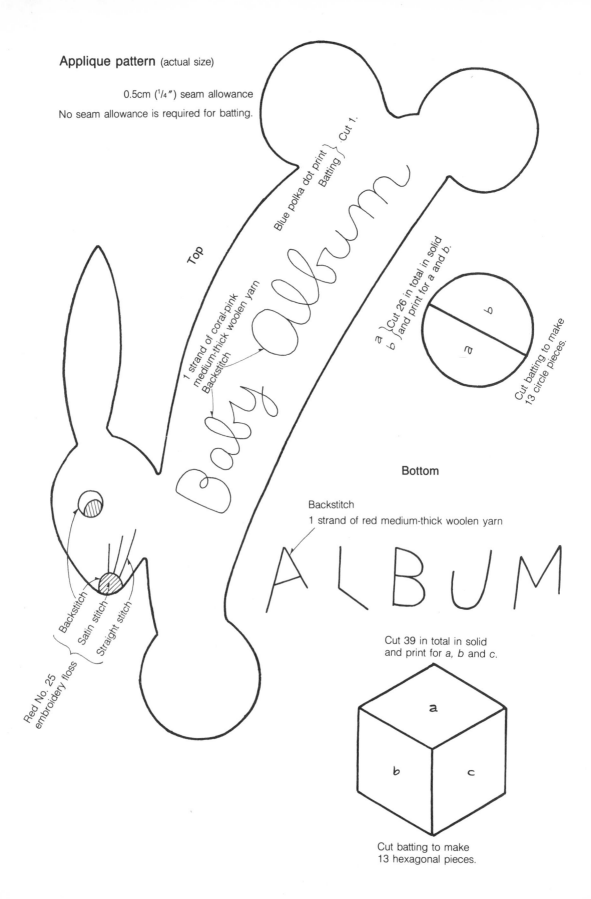

Applique pattern (actual size)

0.5cm (¹/₄″) seam allowance

No seam allowance is required for batting.

Top

Blue polka dot print ⎱ Cut 1.
Batting ⎰

1 strand of coral-pink
medium-thick woolen yarn
Backstitch

a ⎱ Cut 26 in total in solid
b ⎰ and print for a and b.

Cut batting to make
13 circle pieces.

b

a

Bottom

Backstitch
1 strand of red medium-thick woolen yarn

Backstitch
Satin stitch
Straight stitch

Red No. 25
embroidery floss

Baby album

ALBUM

Cut 39 in total in solid
and print for a, b and c.

a

b   c

Cut batting to make
13 hexagonal pieces.

Crib Quilt p.44

Materials: 120cm by 2m ($47^{1}/_{4}'' \times 78^{3}/_{4}''$) white cotton satin. 105cm ($41^{3}/_{4}''$) square white cotton. 105cm ($41^{3}/_{4}''$) batting. 8 skeins of white embroidery floss.

Finished size: 102cm ($40^{1}/_{8}''$) square

Directions: 1. Transfer border wave pattern, embroidery and quilting patterns on top piece. (Enlarge patterns for embroidery and quilting in center to specified size.)
2. Embroider letters with outline stitch.
3. Place batting between top piece and backing, baste in place and quilt, working from center outward.
4. Trim edges to drawn wave line, and finish them with binding.

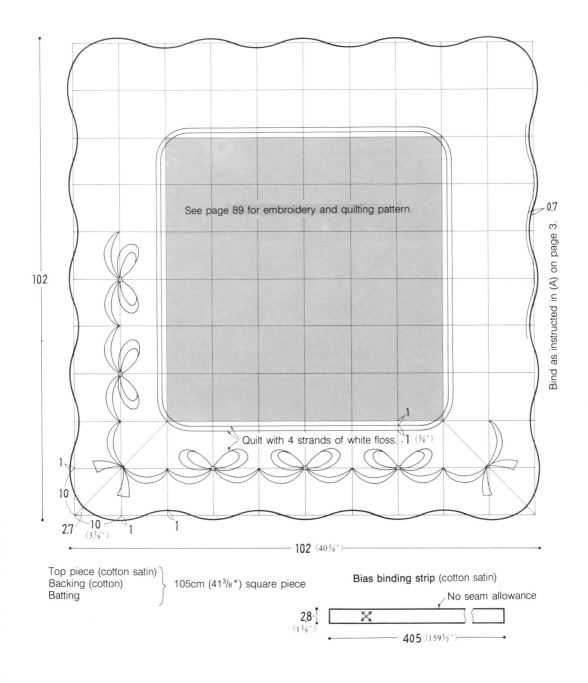

See page 89 for embroidery and quilting pattern.

0.7

Bind as instructed in (A) on page 3.

102

Quilt with 4 strands of white floss. 1 ($^{3}/_{8}''$)

1

1

10

2.7

10 ($^{3}/_{8}''$)

1

1

102 ($40^{1}/_{8}''$)

Top piece (cotton satin)
Backing (cotton) } 105cm ($41^{3}/_{8}''$) square piece
Batting

Bias binding strip (cotton satin)

No seam allowance

28 ($1^{1}/_{8}''$)

405 ($159^{1}/_{2}''$)

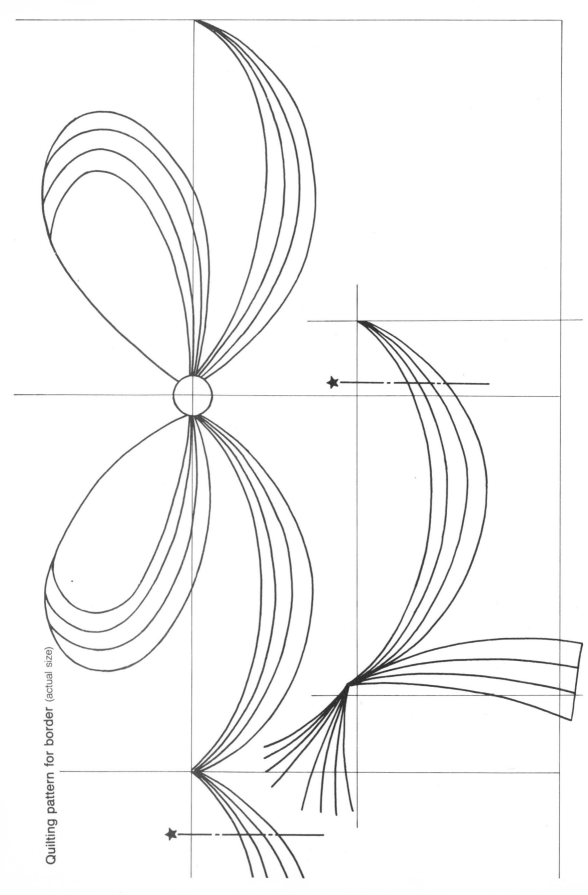

Quilting pattern for border (actual size)

Use 4 strands of white embroidery floss.
Embroider letters with outline stitch.

Baby's Family Tree

Uncle

Aunt

Grand Mother

Grand Father

Grand Mother

Grand Father

Mother

Our Baby

Father

Born on the 10 th of May in 1987
Baby's Birth Weight And Height
3200 g and 50 cm

10 cm

10 cm (3⅞")

Continued from p.51

Embroidery and quilting patterns (actual size)

0.7cm (¼") seam allowance

D Backstitch in 3 strands yellow-brown

Memory

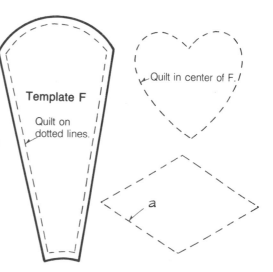

Template F

Quilt on dotted lines.

Quilt in center of F.

a

Tea Cozy p.49

Materials: 47cm by 58cm ($18^{1}/_{2}'' \times 22^{7}/_{8}''$) red prequilted gingham. Assorted solid, checkered and striped red cotton scraps (18 patch pieces of 7cm ($2^{3}/_{4}''$) square). 7cm by 4cm ($2^{3}/_{4}'' \times 1^{5}/_{8}''$) cotton scrap for loop.

Directions: With right sides together, seam front and back pieces, setting a loop between. Turn right sides out, turn inside lower edges and stitch. Cut and join patch pieces, and attach pieced strips to front and back pieces with machine-stitch.

Finish raw edges of prequilted gingham fabric with overcasting-stitch.

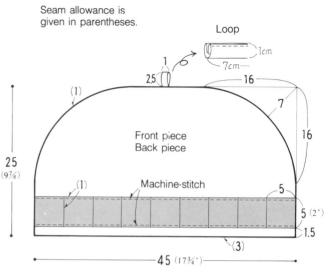

Seam allowance is given in parentheses.

Loop

Front piece
Back piece

Machine-stitch

25 ($9^{7}/_{8}$)

45 ($17^{3}/_{4}''$)

Cut 18 patch pieces in total in solid, checkered and striped.
Cut 7cm by 4cm ($2^{3}/_{4}'' \times 1^{5}/_{8}''$) piece for loop.

Place Mats p.49

Materials for 1 placemat: 70cm by 50cm ($27^{1}/_{2}'' \times 19^{5}/_{8}''$) prequilted gingham (*Top:* red, *Bottom:* dark blue). Assorted solid, checkered and striped cotton scraps for patch pieces (*Top:* red-and-white, *Bottom:* dark blue-and-white).

Finished size: 48cm by 33cm ($18^{7}/_{8}'' \times 13''$)
Directions: Cut and join patch pieces by machine. Lay pieced top on foundation and topstitch along edges. With right sides together, seam top piece and backing, tucking in seam allowance.

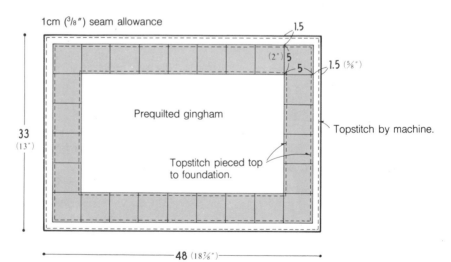

1cm ($^{3}/_{8}''$) seam allowance

Prequilted gingham

Topstitch pieced top to foundation.

Topstitch by machine.

33 (13″)

48 ($18^{7}/_{8}''$)

Cut 26 pieces of 7cm ($2^{3}/_{4}''$) square in assorted solid, checkered and striped (Top: red; Bottom: dark blue)
Cut prequilted gingham to make a piece 50cm by 35cm ($19^{5}/_{8}'' \times 13^{3}/_{4}''$) for backing.

Continued from p.47

Applique pattern (actual size)

D
Cut 3.

E
Cut 3.

Seamline of patch
pieces *b and c*

Tablecloth pp.52,53

Materials: 74cm by 328cm (29¹/₈″ × 129¹/₈″) oyster-white cotton. Assorted print cotton scraps for patch pieces. 65cm by 328cm (25⁵/₈″ × 129¹/₇″) backing.

Finished size: 162cm by 125cm (63³/₄″ × 49¹/₄″)

Directions: 1. Cut and join patch pieces (*a, b* and *c*). Join blocks together and then to oyster-white cotton piece.

2. With right sides together, seam top piece and backing, leaving an opening for turning.

3. Quilt as shown and topstitch along edges by machine.

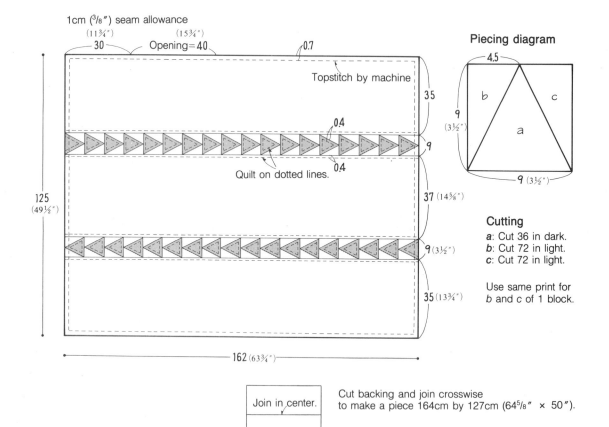

1cm (³/₈″) seam allowance

(11¾″) (15¾″)
30 — Opening=40 — 0.7

Topstitch by machine

35

9 (3½″)

0.4

Quilt on dotted lines. 0.4

125 (49½″)

37 (14⅝″)

9 (3½″)

35 (13¾″)

162 (63¾″)

Piecing diagram

4.5

b *c*

a

9 (3½″)

9 (3½″)

Cutting

a: Cut 36 in dark.
b: Cut 72 in light.
c: Cut 72 in light.

Use same print for *b* and *c* of 1 block.

Join in center.

Cut backing and join crosswise to make a piece 164cm by 127cm (64⁵/₈″ × 50″).

Potholders pp.60,61

Materials: *Top:* 35cm (13³/₄″) square rose-pink cotton, 20cm (7⁷/₈″) square red print cotton, 20cm square red checkered cotton, 21cm by 20cm (8¹/₄″ × 7⁷/₈″) prequilted unbleached cotton.

Bottom: 35cm (13³/₄″) square orange cotton, 20cm (7⁷/₈″) square yellow cotton, 20cm square orange-and-white polka dot cotton, 21cm by 20cm (8¹/₄″ × 7⁷/₈″) prequilted yellow cotton.

Directions: 1. Cut and join patch pieces (*a-e*), lay pieced top on prequilted backing and baste it in place.

2. Finish lower edges of front and back pieces with binding strip *A* respectively.

3. With wrong sides of front and back pieces together, trim upper edges of prequilted pieces to size of pieced top. Finish edges with binding strip *B*, setting a loop in position.

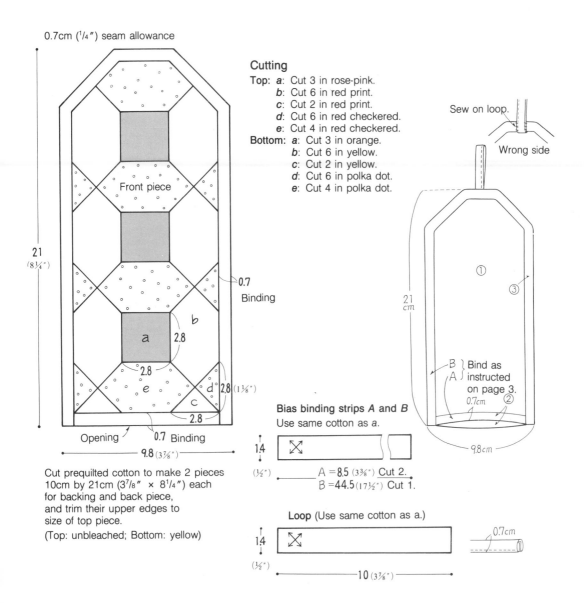

0.7cm (¼″) seam allowance

Cutting

Top: *a*: Cut 3 in rose-pink.
     b: Cut 6 in red print.
     c: Cut 2 in red print.
     d: Cut 6 in red checkered.
     e: Cut 4 in red checkered.

Bottom: *a*: Cut 3 in orange.
     b: Cut 6 in yellow.
     c: Cut 2 in yellow.
     d: Cut 6 in polka dot.
     e: Cut 4 in polka dot.

Front piece

21 (8¼″)

0.7 Binding

Opening   0.7 Binding

9.8 (3⅞″)

2.8

2.8

2.8

2.8 (1⅛″)

a   b   c   d   e

Sew on loop.

Wrong side

21 cm

9.8 cm

B ⎱ Bind as
A ⎰ instructed
on page 3.
0.7cm

① ② ③

Cut prequilted cotton to make 2 pieces
10cm by 21cm (3⅞″ × 8¼″) each
for backing and back piece,
and trim their upper edges to
size of top piece.

(Top: unbleached; Bottom: yellow)

Bias binding strips *A* and *B*
Use same cotton as *a*.

14 (½″)

A = 8.5 (3⅜″) Cut 2.
B = 44.5 (17½″) Cut 1.

Loop (Use same cotton as *a*.)

14 (½″)

0.7cm

10 (3⅞″)

Pot Mats p.60,61

Materials: *Left:* 30cm by 10cm (11¾″ × 3⅞″)
light pink cotton, 35cm by 10cm (13¾″ × 3⅞″)
red checkered cotton, 40cm by 25cm (15¾″ ×
9⅞″) rose-pink cotton, 13cm by 5cm (5⅛″ × 2″)
pink cotton. 20cm (7⅞″) square batting. Pink No.
25 embroidery floss. *Right:* 30cm by 10cm (11¾″ ×
3⅞″) light blue cotton, 35cm by 10cm (13¾″ ×
3⅞″) blue print cotton, 40cm by 25cm (15¾″ ×
9⅞″) blue cotton, 13cm by 5cm (5⅛″ × 2″)

peacock-blue print. 20cm (7⅞″) batting. Blue No.
25 embroidery floss.
Finished size: 20cm (7⅞″) square
Directions: Cut and join patch pieces (*a-h*). With right
sides together, seam pieced top and backing, leaving
an opening for turning. Turn right sides out, laying
batting between, and slipstitch opening. Quilt with
2 strands of embroidery floss as shown.

Piecing diagram
0.5cm seam allowance

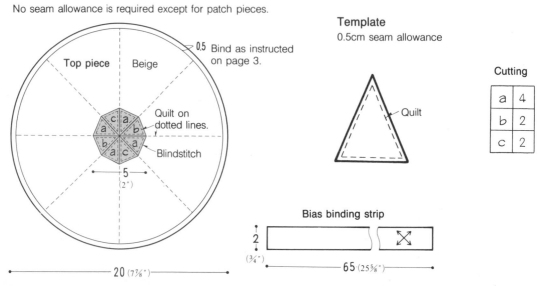

Cutting

Left: *a*: Cut 2 in light pink.
b: Cut 2 in checkered.
c: Cut 4 in rose-pink.
d: Cut 4 in pink.
e: Cut 4 in light pink.
f: Cut 8 in light pink.
g: Cut 8 in checkered.
h: Cut 8 in rose-pink.

Right: *a*: Cut 2 in light blue.
b: Cut 2 in print.
c: Cut 4 in blue.
d: Cut 4 in peacock-blue.
e: Cut 4 in light blue.
f: Cut 8 in light blue.
g: Cut 8 in print.
h: Cut 8 in blue.

Left: Quilt in pink.   *Right*: Quilt in blue.

Cut batting to make a piece 20cm (7⁷/₈″) square.
Cut backing (same cotton as c) to make a piece 21cm
(8¹/₄″) square.

Plate Mats p.56

Materials for 1 platemat: 60cm by 50cm (23⁵/₈″ × 19⁵/₈″) beige cotton. Assorted print cotton scraps. 20cm (7⁷/₈″) square batting.
Finished size: 20cm (7⁷/₈″) in diameter

Directions: Cut and join patch pieces (*a, b* and *c*). Lay pieced block in center of top piece and blindstitch. Place batting between top piece and backing, and finish edges with binding.

No seam allowance is required except for patch pieces.

0.5 Bind as instructed on page 3.

Top piece | Beige

Quilt on dotted lines.

Blindstitch

Quilt on dotted lines.

5 (2″)

20 (7⁷/₈″)

Template
0.5cm seam allowance

Quilt

Cutting

a	4
b	2
c	2

Bias binding strip

2 (³/₄″)

65 (25⁵/₈″)

Cut backing (in beige) and batting to make
a circle piece of 20cm (7⁷/₈″) in diameter respectively.

Basic Embroidery Stitches

Satin Stitch

Outline Stitch

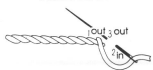

1 out 3 out
2 in

Chain Stitch

Lazy Daisy Stitch

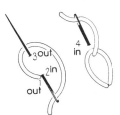

3 out
4 in
2 in
1 out

Back Stitch

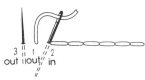

3 out 1 out 2 in

French Knot

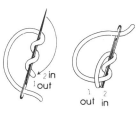

2 in
1 out
1 2
out in

Fly Stitch

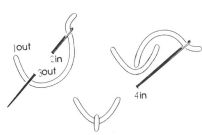

1 out 2 in
3 out
4 in

Running Stitch

4 3 2 1
in out in out

Straight Stitch

1 out 3 out
2 in 4 in

Fern Stitch

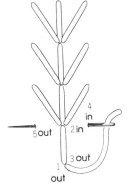

4 in
5 out 2 in
3 out
1 out

Double Cross Stitch

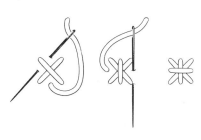

Couching

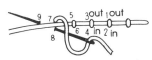

9 7 5 3 out 1 out
8 6 4 in 2 in

Seed Filling Stitch

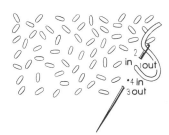

2 in 1 out
•4 in 3 out

Open Buttonhole Stitch

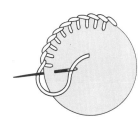